HIGHER
Business Management

Homework Activities

Honor Savage

Consultant Alistair Wylie

HODDER
GIBSON
AN HACHETTE UK COMPANY

The Publishers would like to thank the following for permission to reproduce copyright material:

Photo credits
Page 2 © MBI/Alamy; Page 4 © Cultura/Alamy; Page 6 © Pierre Arsenault/Alamy; Page 8 © mediacolor's/Alamy; Page 10 © 2009 photolibrary.com; Page 12 © Ingram Publishing Limited; Page 14 © Monalyn Gracia/Corbis; Page 16 © Katharine Andriotis Photography, LLC/Alamy; Page 18 © Monalyn Gracia/Corbis; Page 20 © John Davies/ photographersdirect.com; Page 22 © Larry Lilac/Alamy; Page 24 © 2009 photolibrary.com; Page 26 © Christopher Furlong/Getty Images; Page 28 © Patrice Latron/Corbis; Page 30 © Richard Naude/Alamy; Page 32 © Frederic Pitchal/ Sygma/Corbis; Page 34 © Jason Alden/Rex Features; Page 36 © Tetra Images/Alamy; Page 38 © MBI/Alamy; Page 40 © PhotoAlto/Alamy; Page 42 © 2009 photolibrary.com; Page 44 © Masterfile/Radius Images/Corbis; Page 46 © Sean Murphy/Stone/Getty Images; Page 48 © Helene Rogers/Alamy; Page 50 © Chloe Johnson/Alamy; Page 52 © Graeme Robertson/Getty Images; Page 54 © Caro/Alamy.

Acknowledgements
Every effort has been made to trace all copyright holders, but if any have been inadvertently overlooked the Publishers will be pleased to make the necessary arrangements at the first opportunity.

Although every effort has been made to ensure that website addresses are correct at time of going to press, Hodder Gibson cannot be held responsible for the content of any website mentioned in this book. It is sometimes possible to find a relocated web page by typing in the address of the home page for a website in the URL window of your browser.

Hachette's policy is to use papers that are natural, renewable and recyclable products and made from wood grown in sustainable forests. The logging and manufacturing processes are expected to conform to the environmental regulations of the country of origin.

Orders: please contact Bookpoint Ltd, 130 Milton Park, Abingdon, Oxon OX14 4SB. Telephone: (44) 01235 827720. Fax: (44) 01235 400454. Lines are open 9.00 – 5.00, Monday to Saturday, with a 24-hour message answering service. Visit our website at www.hoddereducation.co.uk. Hodder Gibson can be contacted direct on: Tel: 0141 848 1609; Fax: 0141 889 6315; email: hoddergibson@hodder.co.uk

Cover photos © Brownstock Inc./Alamy and © Andy Arthur/Alamy
Typeset in 10.5/13pt Berling and 10/13pt Myriad by Dorchester Typesetting Group
Printed by MPG Books Ltd, Bodmin

A catalogue record for this title is available from the British Library
ISBN-13: 978 0340 987 582

Contents

Introduction

Welcome to *Higher Business Management Homework Activities*.

This book is intended as a companion to other books from Hodder Gibson supporting the Scottish Qualification Authority's (SQA) courses in Business Management at Higher level.

The book is designed for use by candidates studying the course and working towards the external examination. It provides class work and homework activities that follow the topics and units of the course. Each area of the course is covered by at least one of the activities and this has been referenced on the opposite page.

Each activity is based around a short case study. These have been designed to give candidates ample opportunity to become familiar with a similar format to the external examination and all questions use the recommended command words. At the end of the book, three NAB-style tests have been provided to test consolidated knowledge and learning.

Solutions have been provided to all questions but it should be noted that they do not exemplify the use of the command words and provide a summary of the main points that a marker would expect to find in an answer. They are, therefore, not exhaustive in nature and can act only as a basic check for candidates without the assistance of a teacher.

It is intended that there are sufficient examples in the book to provide approximately one assessment per week to be tackled. Depending on the delivery of the course, these may not necessarily be tackled in the order presented in the book. Whilst the NAB-style tests at the end of the book have 40 marks to mirror the SQA NAB tests, the case studies have questions totalling 25 marks to make them more accessible for the average length of a lesson and also for more frequent homework use.

A very special thanks goes to Alistair Wylie whose belief allowed this book to happen and whose guidance has been invaluable. Also, a special thanks to the staff at Hodder Gibson, in particular, Katherine Bennett for her due diligence and support.

I hope and trust you will this a useful resource during your period of study.

Honor Savage

Topic Frequency

UNIT 1
Case Study 1 Type of business organisation | Sources of assistance and finance | Growth
Case Study 2 Stakeholders | Objectives | Types of sectors
Case Study 3 Franchising | Outsourcing | De-merger | Why grow

UNIT 2
Case Study 1 Types of business information | Sources of finance | External environment
Case Study 2 Sources of information | Uses of information | Legislation of handling data
Case Study 3 ICT to improve communication | Costs and benefits ICT | Factors restricting ICT | Effects of ICT on the firm

UNIT 3
Case Study 1 Types of decisions | SWOT | Internal constraints
Case Study 2 POGADSCIE | Assess decision-making models | External factors
Case Study 3 Roles of managers | Ways to evaluate a decision | ICT and decision-making

UNIT 4
Case Study 1 Organisation groupings | Objectives
Case Study 2 Types of structure | Factors influencing choice of structure | Role of a manager with changes in structure
Case Study 3 Corporate culture | Empowerment

UNIT 5
Case Study 1 Market orientation | Market research | Niche marketing
Case Study 2 Marketing mix | Product and price only | Segmenting the market
Case Study 3 Marketing mix | Promotion and place only | Sponsorship

UNIT 6
Case Study 1 Purchasing | Stock control | JIT | Computerised stock control
Case Study 2 Methods of production | Factors influencing choice of dist channel | ICT and operations
Case Study 3 Quality methods | Methods of payment | Objectives and decisions

UNIT 7
Case Study 1 Contents of trading and P&L account | Balance sheet | Working capital
Case Study 2 Accounting ratios
Case Study 3 Cash flow forecast (budget) | Cash flow statement | Stakeholders interest | Sources of finance

UNIT 8
Case Study 1 Recruitment | Selection
Case Study 2 Induction | Training | Appraisal and motivation
Case Study 3 Employee relations | Industrial relations | Legislative requirements

Business in Contemporary Society: Coffee & Chords

Case Study 1

Gianni and Chiara purchased a small ground level office space next to a local college. In addition to their savings, they obtained a grant from the Princes Trust and decided to open a café, *Coffee & Chords*, which also offered an open mic session for budding musicians at night. This attracted students from the college. They managed to secure their furniture on credit. They leased their catering equipment and all electronic goods were bought on hire purchase from *Comet*.

In the Deed of Partnership, it was agreed that Chiara was in charge of marketing and finance and Gianni took control of the day to day running of the business including the hiring and firing of staff. Profits and losses were to be shared equally.

The café was was so successful that Chiara believed quick growth through the franchising route was a possibility. Locations next to Scottish colleges could be targeted using the same successful format as *Coffee & Chords*, with possible merchandising spin off in the form of mugs, t-shirts etc. A looming recession, however, made Gianni apprehensive as it would be necessary to convert the business to a private limited company to secure more funds.

Gianni's alternative plan was to buy out the café's supplier of food with the possibility of expanding the café into a restaurant. The supplier's food prices were high, deliveries were often late to the café and invoicing problems were resulting in cashflow problems. Buying out the supplier could reduce these problems, move the business into another area and spread their risk.

Gianni and Chiara decided to hold a meeting to establish a vision for the café, before drafting a business plan for the bank manager with the intention of asking for a bank loan.

Questions

Write your ideas about each question in note form on the lines provided. You should then write out your full answers to this Case Study on a fresh piece of paper.

1. Under the heading of "External Factors", identify the problems for *Coffee & Chords*. *3 marks*

2. Gianni and Chiara are a partnership but may have to change to a private limited company. Compare these types of business organisations. *4 marks*

3. (a) Describe and justify the 3 sources of finance that Chiara and Gianni accessed to set up the business. *6 marks*

   (b) In addition to the Princes Trust, identify 2 forms of financial assistance Chiara and Gianni could have accessed at the start-up of their business. *2 marks*

4. Gianni and Chiara could be described as entrepreneurs. Describe 4 characteristics of an entrepreneur. *4 marks*

5. (a) Identify the method of growth that Gianni wanted to follow. *1 mark*

   (b) Discuss the advantages and disadvantages of this form of growth. *5 marks*

25 marks

Business in Contemporary Society: Coffee & Chords

Case Study 2

When running their café, *Coffee & Chords*, Gianni and Chiara had to deal with several stakeholders who had both an interest and influence on their business.

The bank had given Chiara advice on the costs involved in converting the business to a franchise. Their solicitors, Sue & Run, had explained the legalities involved. Chiara was made aware of the franchisees' rights in running the business, such as terminating contracts. As their café was in a listed building, Gianni and Chiara had sought planning permission when making alterations to the front of their business. Gianni and Chiara had promised the local community that the café would be properly sound-proofed and any changes would improve the appearance of the street.

The café was very successful and a loyal client base formed. Artists from the design course at the college were keen to display their work in the café. A local taxi firm installed a free phone offering a direct line to their taxi base. Gianni and Chiara bought advertising space in the college paper. In order to stay ahead of the competition Gianni and Chiara sought ideas for theme nights from their staff. As a result of being in tune with their local customers the café was able to open longer and existing staff were offered more hours. The competing cafés just seemed to look on in amazement at the success of the business.

For Gianni and Chiara, the success of the café meant they had to change their business goals. At first when money was short and customers had not yet heard of them, the goal of the café was simply to survive. After the first year Gianni and Chiara decided to invest some of their profits into advertising in order to increase sales. When the café finally established a name for itself, Gianni and Chiara started to bring in more expensive food dishes and foreign beers to raise profits.

Questions

Write your ideas about each question in note form on the lines provided. You should then write out your full answers to this Case Study on a fresh piece of paper.

1. (a) Describe the interest 5 stakeholders would have in *Coffee & Chords*.   5 marks

   Expanding, jobs, loans, selling products and entertainments

   (b) Describe the influence 5 stakeholders would have on *Coffee & Chords*. 5 marks

   Help expand, keep running, improve and make better

2. Describe 3 potential conflicts there may have been between the owners of the business and the local community.   3 marks

3. Describe the possible effects of competition on *Coffee & Chords*.   2 marks

   Shutting down, increase prices and sales. Or improve and get more customers.

4. (a) Describe 3 objectives of *Coffee & Chords*.   3 marks

   Maximising profit, growth and survival

   (b) Describe how Gianni and Chiara could find out if their objectives were achieved.   3 marks

   Compare money made, ask employees & customers opinions.

5. The local council is part of the public sector. Describe the advantages a firm in the public sector has over a private sector firm such as *Coffee & Chords*.   4 marks

   25 marks

Business in Contemporary Society: Coffee & Chords

Case Study 3

Gianni and Chiara's decision to franchise the café, *Coffee & Chords*, was a great success. They opened five cafés in a short period of time and achieved many cost savings through bulk buying discounts with their food and furniture and the risks were shared. However, they had problems with the quality of service with some of the franchisees so Chiara took charge of training and drafted a guide on how each franchise was to be run.

Chiara gave up control of the marketing of the café and they decided to outsource their advertising to a well-known advertising agency. This firm was experienced with highly skilled staff. They had many contacts with internet and billboard companies and could advise Gianni and Chiara on the best media to use to suit their client base. This was expensive but overall cheaper for Gianni and Chiara than setting up a marketing department in *Coffee & Chords*. In addition, services were only paid for when required.

Unfortunately, the first advert had taken time to get right and Chiara complained at the loss of control over this important area. Chiara was also uncomfortable with the advertising agency's current dealings with a competitor and feared some private information could be disclosed such as the timings of *Coffee & Chords'* promotional campaigns.

The advertising company itself had just undergone a demerger, from one firm to two separate organisations. The other firm had focused on market research, moved to London and was looking to win the contract for the Olympic Games. The advertising organisation stayed in Scotland, focused on advertising and handled accounts such as *Coffee & Chords*. It allowed them to focus purely on advertising, making for more effective use of staff skills and equipment.

Questions

Write your ideas about each question in note form on the lines provided. You should then write out your full answers to this Case Study on a fresh piece of paper.

1. (a) Describe the term franchising.   *2 marks*

   I firm pays for rights to run under trading name.

   (b) Discuss franchising as a method of growth for a firm such as
       Coffee & Chords.   *6 marks*

2. (a) Describe the term outsourcing.   *2 marks*

   (b) Discuss the advantages and disadvantages to a firm of outsourcing
       some of its activities.   *7 marks*

3. (a) Describe the term de-merger.   *2 marks*

   (b) Explain why a firm might decide to de-merge as a form of growth.   *2 marks*

4. Describe the reasons why a firm such as *Coffee & Chords* would want
   to grow.   *4 marks*

25 marks

Business Information & ICT:
The Phatty

Case Study 1

The Phatty is a local cultural newspaper containing articles of interest on topical issues such as music, sport and going out. The paper is part of a wider publishing group with sales throughout Scotland. One of its editors was concerned, however, at the rise in popularity of the internet and its ability to attract larger advertising revenues.

To this end, he decided to revamp the paper. The articles were changed to contain a selection of graphics and eye-catching pictures alongside typed articles that had been reduced in length to keep the interest of the reader. On one occasion he encouraged a journalist, with his recent article on indie bands, to place the statistics onto a graph that would more clearly show the most popular band across the different cities. Pictures supported the articles alongside responses from leading DJs in a different font size.

In the office, the editor introduced weekly breakfast meetings. These were relaxed, with the focus being to encourage more face to face contact amongst staff, with verbal communication replacing written emails. At one of these meetings the editor was able to circulate a copy of the paper's improved cashflow. At first the group went quiet but, following a few questions from the staff, all workers left the meeting with a clear understanding of a cashflow statement as a forecast of the firm's sales over a period of a year. The figures had also included a "what if scenario" where the group could see the financial implications of investing more money in advertising.

Questions

Write your ideas about each question in note form on the lines provided. You should then write out your full answers to this Case Study on a fresh piece of paper.

1. Describe the advantages to a firm, such as *The Phatty*, of using graphics to illustrate the figures.   *3 marks*

2. Describe the advantages to a firm, such as *The Phatty*, of using pictorial information to communicate to their customers.   *3 marks*

3. Describe the benefits to a firm, such as *The Phatty*, of encouraging verbal communication amongst its staff.   *3 marks*

4. (a) Describe the purpose of a "what if scenario" in relation to spreadsheets.   *2 marks*

    (b) Describe the advantages of using spreadsheets in a business.   *3 marks*

    (c) Describe the advantages of using figures to communicate with employees.   *2 marks*

5. Describe 3 advantages of using written forms of communication instead of verbal communication.   *3 marks*

6. Describe the advantages and disadvantages of 2 forms of finance that a firm, such as *The Phatty*, could have accessed to update its printing machines.   *4 marks*

7. Explain 2 external influences that affected the success of *The Phatty*.   *2 marks*

25 marks

Business Information & ICT:
The Phatty

Case Study 2

The Phatty's move to an e-newspaper was a successful growth strategy where the focus changed to managing information rather than people, which required The Phatty's managers to improve their understanding of handling sources of information.

Primary:

An online survey established a profile of The Phatty's target audience which influenced web links such as ticket agencies for summer festivals. An up to date database of email addresses of The Phatty's client base was used for marketing campaigns. This information kept The Phatty on the pulse of their young audience but response rates to their survey were low and the market research agency's cost to collect and analyse the results was high. The popularity of certain eateries was monitored through the response to promotions and this data was then sold on to the larger pub chains.

Secondary:

To support this primary data, The Phatty relied on social trends to quantify population trends for certain regions. Radio listeners figures were bought from local radio stations which established the size of markets around key towns. University brochures were read to establish the popularity of courses.

Internal:

Within The Phatty, the editors monitored staff performance through response rates to journalists' articles. These were sent via emails to staff who could compare their own performance to the other writers whilst gauging the public's appetite for current issues. Training courses were agreed via email and the parents company's newsletter was communcated in a similar fashion, notifying writers of jobs.

External:

The universities' staff lists were useful when the journalists wanted to consult experts on topical issues such as teenage alcoholism. TV listings allowed journalists to keep abreast of popular current programmes. The accountants constantly measured the rental rates of office properties to ensure costs were minimised. Legal documents such as the Data Protection Act were consulted to ensure the correct handling of all their readers' data and competitors' websites were trawled for new ideas.

Questions

Write your ideas about each question in note form on the lines provided. You should then write out your full answers to this Case Study on a fresh piece of paper.

1. Explain how firms such as *The Phatty* could use primary information to enhance the performance of their business.

   4 marks

2. Explain the value of the secondary information collected by a firm such as *The Phatty*.

   6 marks

3. Explain how *The Phatty* used the various sources of information to enhance the following areas of the business:
   - decision-making
   - identifying new business opportunities
   - measuring the performance of the business
   - monitoring the performance of the firm

   4 marks

4. Discuss the value of internal and external information used to improve the performance of the business.

   6 marks

5. Describe the legal demands that firms such as *The Phatty* will have to follow when handling the information collected.

   5 marks

   25 marks

Business Information & ICT:
The Phatty

Case Study 3

The journalists of *The Phatty*, a cultural newspaper for young people, had just learned, via a powerpoint presentation by their editor, that the firm would be following an objective of growth. This would be achieved by changing the paper version of *The Phatty* to an internet magazine (e-zine). The growing trend of viewing newspapers online and *The Phatty*'s target audience of computer literate students made it an excellent business to trial this new venture.

The initial layout of the website had been difficult to establish and required several video conference meetings between the editors (Dundee-based) and the (Swindon-based) ICT company, contracted in to deal with the ICT requirements. Many emails had passed between the firms, sorting out which links to introduce and also agreeing security measures for online subscribers. The offices for *The Phatty*'s staff had changed location and downsized considerably as many of the editors preferred the option of teleworking. The production staff who were selected for redundancy were offered training to enhance their ICT skills and, despite threats of job losses, many changed roles to become website managers.

It was hoped the website would virtually pay for itself through advertising revenue. Package deals were offered to larger fast food chains for homepage pop-up ads, with smaller businesses such as local restaurants being sold space on local links for events such as music festivals. The reduction in paper consumption won *The Phatty* an award from an environmentalist group.

The editor of the website was instructed to monitor the number of hits on various pages which would be an indication of their popularity. Online surveys would help measure the target audience response to *The Phatty* and the subsequent collection of email addresses would be used for future advertising campaigns.

Questions

Write your ideas about each question in note form on the lines provided. You should then write out your full answers to this Case Study on a fresh piece of paper.

1. Explain the ways in which *The Phatty* used ICT to improve communication in its business.   *7 marks*

2. Discuss the costs and benefits to a firm such as *The Phatty* when introducing ICT.   *8 marks*

3. Describe the factors that might restrict a firm's use of modern technology.   *4 marks*

4. Describe the effects of introducing ICT on a) the staff and b) the firm.   *6 marks*

25 marks

Decision-making:
Head2Head

Case Study 1

Donna and Craig own a small chain of hairdressing salons, *Head2Head*. Business has been good and the couple are faced with many decisions about their future.

Craig has set the main aim of the business as growth. He wants to achieve this by expanding the male client base in light of the rise in male grooming. Before approaching the bank for the extra finance for this expansion, Donna and Craig decide to do a SWOT on the business. Their strengths, it is revealed, are their reputable brand name and low prices. Their weaknesses are their relative inexperience, a lack of skilled staff to step in as managers and a shortage of cash.

The external business has shown a gap in the market for hairdressers offering a range of services for men. A recent London survey had shown a demand for this service but a reluctance of most men to visit the mainly female orientated outlets. The threats of this venture would come from the larger chains who have the financial clout and management expertise to copy their idea quickly. A recession was also looming.

On the conclusions drawn from the SWOT, Donna and Craig decided to proceed with the venture. Donna, as head stylist would draw up their objectives for the bank. Craig, with his contacts, would be in charge of buying all the equipment and arranging the advertising for the salons. Once set up, Donna would manage the rota for staff on a daily basis. In keeping with most barbers they would not have a booking system and instead deal with clients as they appeared.

After the first year, Donna and Craig were facing closure.

Questions

Write your ideas about each question in note form on the lines provided. You should then write out your full answers to this Case Study on a fresh piece of paper.

1. Under the heading, "External Factors", identify the problems *Head2Head* are facing.   *4 marks*

2. Describe 3 different types of decisions made by Donna and Craig to change their business.   *6 marks*

3. Describe the results of the SWOT analysis that Donna and Craig conducted on their business.   *8 marks*

4. Discuss whether or not the results of the SWOT analysis justified Donna and Craig's decision to expand the business at this time?   *2 marks*

5. Describe the internal constraints that might have prevented Donna and Craig from making a good decision.   *5 marks*

25 marks

Decision-making:
Head2Head

Case Study 2

Donna and Craig's decision to expand *Head2Head*, their existing small chain of hairdressing salons, into the male grooming market was not successful. They had failed to break even, profits were down and customers complaints on the standard of service were up. The recession was in full flow and the press were critical of many leading males' preoccupation with their appearance at the expense of their sports commitments.

They sought advice from a management consultant who submitted the following conclusions:

- There were no clear objectives set for their venture.
- They had failed to gather the right information on customer opinions, competitors, and equipment costs.
- No alternatives, such as a gradual introduction of the male grooming idea, were considered.
- Staff were kept out of the decision and so failed to get the proper training to acquire new skills.
- Donna and Craig's adverts were placed in an evening daily newspaper as opposed to gyms where their target audience clustered.
- There was little attempt to forecast demand and negotiate price discounts with suppliers leaving them with a lot of unsold, expensive stock.

Overall, decisions had been made in haste and lacked proper planning. Staff were kept in the dark and decisions were made on hunches as opposed to good market information.

All was not lost and Donna and Craig were advised to undertake the following:
- Use a decison-making model such as POGADSCIE to force the firm to consider alternatives.
- Consult with business advisors such as Business Gateway and get advice on handling big decisions and implementing change in the business.
- Create a culture within the business where staff are consulted and encouraged to give their ideas on the direction of the business.

Questions

Write your ideas about each question in note form on the lines provided. You should then write out your full answers to this Case Study on a fresh piece of paper.

1. Using the decision-making model "POGADSCIE", describe how Donna and Craig might have reached the decision to enter the male grooming market.
   9 marks

2. Explain the advantages to a firm, such as *Head2Head*, of using a decision-making model when making a decision.
   4 marks

3. Explain the disadvantages to a firm, such as *Head2Head*, of using a decision-making model for every decision.
   4 marks

4. Describe the factors that a business could introduce to ensure quality decisions are made.
   5 marks

5. Describe the external factors that could have contributed to *Head2Head*'s poor performance.
   3 marks

   25 marks

Decision-making:
Head2Head

Case Study 3

Following a brainstorming session on ways to improve their new venture (to develop the male grooming side of their hairdressing business), Donna and Craig began their planning by setting an objective to increase sales by 5 % over the next 2 years. To do this, Craig would have to take a more active role in monitoring the sales performance of each of the shops to give him better control of their performance. He could outline the staff rota one month in advance to allow for changes due to requests for staff absences (command).

Donna would have to coordinate activity across all the shops to manage a concerted effort by everyone to improve service and reach their target of obtaining 10 new male clients each week. Staff could be motivated to reach this goal by awarding the winning salon with a bottle of champagne. She also planned to improve the overall organisation and ensure each salon had the correct stocks of shampoo, lotions and towels.

Donna made use of her staff by delegating the role of training to her head beauticians. They took responsibilitiy for ensuring all junior beauticians had the right skills and approach for the male clients.

The revised approach was an instant success. A database showed they reached their target of obtaining an increase in male clients across all salons. A computerised database of all salon stock levels showed a decrease in stock being thrown out and being stolen. Till receipts showed that sales were up, the website showed the number of customer complaints decreased and they received a good review in an e-commerce magazine, *The Phatty*, for their quality of service. All staff had received accreditation for their training and, despite the increased training costs, profits rose.

Questions

Write your ideas about each question in note form on the lines provided. You should then write out your full answers to this Case Study on a fresh piece of paper.

1. Describe the role of a manager in a firm such as *Head2Head*.   *8 marks*

2. Explain how Donna and Craig could measure the effectiveness of their decisions.   *5 marks*

3. Describe 3 types of decisions made by Donna and Craig, to improve the performance of *Head2Head*.   *6 marks*

4. Explain how ICT might improve decision-making in a firm such as *Head2Head*.   *6 marks*

25 marks

Internal Organisation:
SmoothEEz

Case Study 1

Adam, David and Fiona decided to exploit the trend for healthy drinks and invest their business skills into developing a drink made from yogurt and fruit, which they called *SmoothEEz*.

Adam had studied accountancy and specialised in finance, Fiona managed the marketing and David took responsibility for operations. This created departments and the business took on a functional grouping. David attended courses on improving quality on the production lines and Adam became an expert on ICT accounting packages. Communication, initially, was good as they had clear roles and they all shared the same office. But, as the firm expanded the operations moved to a bigger factory and larger office premises were leased. Re-grouping of the staff would be necessary and Adam thought he had the answer.

During a recent video conference meeting, Adam revealed that 70 % of their business was taken up by three main clients. These comprised a major wholesaler who sold on to the small retailers, a large fast food chain and a supermarket where *SmoothEEz* sold under the supermarket's value brand name. Each client had their unique demands:
- The supermarket required their drinks to be packaged with their own signage.
- The fast food chain required deliveries direct to their warehouses with strict quality checks.
- The wholesaler simply needed *SmoothEEz* to promote the brand to generate good sales.

Adam's proposal was to recommend *SmoothEEz* switch to a customer focused grouping, where a team of staff (division) would be dedicated to meeting each of the main client's needs. Changes, such as a unique invoicing and purchasing system, would be introduced, which could track, for instance, the delivery status of each client's order. Staff and clients could develop brands and promotional campaigns together and staff looking after the supermarket could acquire skills in analysing in-store card research data. Improved client loyalty would also be secured.

Adam warned that costs would rise after the re-structure as marketing would have to be staffed for each of the clients. Economies of scale in bulk buying packaging, for instance, would be lost as each client had their own unique design. Switching staff across each client during busy spells or covering for an absent colleague could also be problematic.

Questions

Write your ideas about each question in note form on the lines provided. You should then write out your full answers to this Case Study on a fresh piece of paper.

1. Describe the objectives *SmoothEEz* might have selected at the start of their venture. *4 marks*

2. Discuss the advantages and disadvantages of *SmoothEEz*'s original type of functional grouping. *6 marks*

3. (a) Describe 2 factors that encouraged *SmoothEEz* to change this grouping to a customer focused grouping. *2 marks*

   (b) Discuss the advantages and disadvantages to Adam's proposal of changing the firm to a customer grouping arrangement. *6 marks*

4. (a) Describe a product or service grouping. *1 mark*

   (b) Discuss this type of grouping for a firm such as *SmoothEEz*. *6 marks*

25 marks

Internal Organisation:
SmoothEEz

Case Study 2

In the early days, *SmoothEEz*, a healthy drinks firm, had formed an entrepreneurial structure with all of the decisions being made by the founders, Adam, David and Fiona. As the firm grew, more departments were created and the firm quickly changed to a hierarchical structure. Communication had slowed with information being passed though an increasing number of layers of management. Decisions took longer to be approved and *SmoothEEz* felt it was losing touch with their customers' needs.

The hierarchical structure required that *SmoothEEz* group staff into departments. However, as *SmoothEEz* expanded further, they changed to a customer grouping which created divisions dedicated to each of their main clients. These divisions proved ideal for flattening the structure through delayering. Each division had fewer layers of management and a shorter chain of command. Staff had more opportunities for face to face contact and communication was quickened. Departments were granted greater autonomy to make decisions on packaging and credit terms that met the individual needs of their client. Managers responded quickly to changes in the market place with new flavours and quirky marketing ideas. However, with the span of control for each divisional manager widening, stress levels began to rise.

SmoothEEz decided to remove some responsibilities from the divisions and centralise a few activities at their Aberdeen Head Office such as Human Resources and Purchasing. This allowed *SmoothEEz* to keep control of recruitment as training specialists were hired. It also meant staff could promote a clear corporate image across all clients. There was centralised purchasing of major items such as fruit to obtain large price discounts and ensure quality. A few major TV adverts were also arranged by Head Office which were popular in the north of Scotland but failed to appeal to customers in the central belt.

Questions

Write your ideas about each question in note form on the lines provided. You should then write out your full answers to this Case Study on a fresh piece of paper.

1. Describe an entrepreneurial structure and the advantages to a firm, such as *SmoothEEz*, of having this structure.   *4 marks*

2. Discuss the decision of a firm, such as *SmoothEEz*, to introduce a hierarchical structure.   *4 marks*

3. Explain the advantages to a firm, such as *SmoothEEz*, of changing to a flatter structure by delayering.   *4 marks*

4. Describe 2 factors that might influence a firm's choice of organisation structure.   *3 marks*

5. Describe the advantages and disadvantages to a firm such as *SmoothEEz* of centralising some of their activities.   *6 marks*

6. Describe the role and responsibility of a manager, such as Adam, when making changes to a firm's structure.   *4 marks*

25 marks

Internal Organisation:
SmoothEEz

Case Study 3

Such was the popularity of their drink *SmoothEEz* that its founders, Adam, David and Fiona decided to open a small chain of cafes called *MilkEE Barz*, aimed purely at younger teenagers. A full range of *SmoothEEz* would be sold in addition to sweets and cakes, but no coffee. This form of forward vertical integration would guarantee a sales outlet of *SmoothEEz*'s drinks whilst allowing contol over the firm's image and the chance to create a distinctive corporate culture.

The *MilkEE Barz* culture was to be common across all outlets: fun, lively and adult-free. Fiona drafted the design of the logo, a cartoon black and white cow, which appeared on mugs, posters and staff uniforms. The seating was low comfy sofas, in the black and white colour theme of the logo. A *MilkEE Barz* e-newsletter was set up where staff could read ideas from other Scottish *MilkEE Barz* and staff were kept informed of the company's performance. Staff training focused on dealing with the younger audience through workshops and DVDs. Overall, it was a great success, especially the inter-cafe competition that built strong bonds amongst staff as they willingly covered shifts in an attempt to win the holiday to Barcelona for the cafe with the highest sales.

Tha aim of Fiona's training was not just to promote a corporate culture but to empower the staff. Staff, through greater access to information, were encouraged to take on more decision-making. Each manager of a *MilkEE Barz* was entrusted to:
- decide their weekly order of *SmoothEEz*, cakes and sweets in response to their customer demands
- monitor staff in terms of time-keeping and quality of service
- design in-store publicity depending on their customers e.g. inner city, shopping centre

Decison-making was more effective as it met the local needs. Staff enjoyed the freedom to design their own publicity and one staff member had their idea for a *SmoothEEz* flavour adopted by the firm. Costs did, however, increase to train the staff and many of the part time members of staff were reluctant to take on any extra responsibility without receiving extra payment.

Questions

Write your ideas about each question in note form on the lines provided. You should then write out your full answers to this Case Study on a fresh piece of paper.

1. (a) Describe the term corporate culture. *2 marks*

   (b) Describe how a firm, such as *SmoothEEz*, could ensure their firm has a strong corporate culture. *5 marks*

   (c) Explain the advantages to firm, such as *SmoothEEz*, of having a strong corporate culture. *5 marks*

2. (a) Describe the term empowerment. *2 marks*

   (b) Describe the ways a firm, such as *SmoothEEz*, could empower its staff. *3 marks*

   (c) Explain the benefits to a firm such as *SmoothEEz* of empowering their staff. *5 marks*

   (d) Describe the possible limitations to a firm, such as *SmoothEEz*, when deciding to empower its staff. *3 marks*

   25 marks

Marketing:
T in the Bag

Case Study 1

On the train back from Scotland's biggest music festival, Alistair, Shazia and Suzy shared photos of their experiences. They had seen many bands and met loads of students from abroad. "I'd liked to have swapped something with them as a momento" said Suzy. "Yeah" agreed Alistair, "something like a customised t-shirt." And so the idea was born. By the time the train had pulled into their home city, the three had formed a marketing plan to set up a t-shirt business.

As the biggest investor, Alistair wanted figures to prove if any profit could be made and so undertook some desk research. He checked the websites of the ticket agencies and the actual festivals to gauge ticket sales and establish a rough level of demand. He visited the music shops to check out the prices of t-shirts and gained the estimated production costs from a manufacturer's catalogue. After doing a quick calculation of potential profit they all agreed the venture was a viable option.

Shazia insisted the company be market-led, "No 'one-size fits all' here." she promised. So putting the customers' views at the centre of the business, she took charge of field research. Her postal survey, although cheap, had a low response rate, so she phoned a few students from lists purchased from universities. This method was again cheap and she was able to cover the whole of Britain, but customers' ideas for designs were difficut to explain over the phone and many students disliked being interupted during their leisure time. In the college canteens, Shazia arranged some focus groups. Opinions and ideas flowed about the styles of t-shirts, for instance, customising each t-shirt with a photo of the customer at the festival. She observed, also, how colour was more important to females and necklines to males.

Test marketing their idea at Scotland's flagship festival gave them the idea of the brand name: *T in the Bag*. They monitored to see if prices were too high, identified the popular styles and sizes and evaluated the effectiveness of advertising. They also alerted customers to their website for future ordering and encouraged online surveys with free tickets for concerts. Suzy was convinced their idea would create a niche market, so prices could be raised and competitors would not see them as a threat.

Questions

Write your ideas about each question in note form on the lines provided. You should then write out your full answers to this Case Study on a fresh piece of paper.

1. (a) Explain the term "market-led". 2 marks

    (b) Explain the benefits to *T in the Bag* of taking this approach to their business. 3 marks

2. (a) Describe, using examples, 4 methods of field research that a firm, such as *T in the Bag*, could use to gather information on their business. 4 marks

    (b) Discuss the advantages and disadvantages of each of the forms of research described in question 2(a). 8 marks

3. (a) Describe, using an example, the term desk research. 2 marks

    (b) Explain the value of information from desk research to Alistair. 2 marks

4. Describe the costs and benefits of a niche market to a firm, such as *T in the Bag*. 4 marks

25 marks

Marketing:
T in the Bag

Case Study 2

Alistair, Shazia and Suzy met up to discuss progress of their quirky t-shirt range called, *T in the Bag*. A few marketing problems had surfaced and Alistair was keen to get them resolved.

Shazia believed the product range was too wide as some designs had been left unsold. The packaging of the t-shirt, called the T-bag, inspired by the music festival T in the Park, was key to their brand and had allowed a premium price to be set. A loyal group of customers was forming with some collecting t-shirts for all the festivals attended that year. Shazia explained that the original t-shirt was moving out of the maturity stage of the product life cycle and so some extension strategies were needed. Suzy thought they could now sell to sports outlets and Alistair suggested some product line extensions such as a festival clothing range, which would build on their already estabished brand name. The T-bag, packaging could be lined with a water-proof and fleece layer and double up as pillow slip and protect against rain showers at the festivals.

Their current price was too high. When it was first released, as a designer product, it secured a high price. But now, with a loyal set of customers and copycat products sure to follow, its price could be lowered. Suzy saw potential with the collectors of t-shirts and suggested a promotional pricing strategy for volume purchases. The problem of unsold stock could be boosted by this pricing method with no loss of quality to the product. Shazia's range of "eco" t-shirts called "Herbal-Ts", could be sold as a loss leader, simply to encourage customers to visit their website and purchase their more profitable ranges. Suzy advised that t-shirts sold via the sports shops should be priced competitively, alongside the leading brands to avoid a price war. They could compete on non-pricing factors such as their distinctive packaging and word of mouth promotions.

Their main problem, concluded Alistair, was poor market research as an inadequate amount of data on their customers had been collected, making segmenting the market difficult. They had failed, for instance, to maximise sales by using a range of pricing strategies targeted at the appropriate customer.

Questions

Write your ideas about each question in note form on the lines provided. You should then write out your full answers to this Case Study on a fresh piece of paper.

1. Under the heading "Marketing", identify the problems *T in the Bag* was facing after its first year of trading.   *4 marks*

2. (a) Describe the costs and benefits of holding a brand name.   *4 marks*

    (b) Describe, using examples, 2 extension strategies a firm, such as *T in the Bag*, could use to extend the life cycle of their product.   *4 marks*

    (c) Explain the advantages to a firm, such as *T in the Bag*, of having a portfolio of products.   *3 marks*

3. (a) Describe 2 pricing strategies a firm, such as *T in the Bag*, could use to maximise its sales.   *4 marks*

    (b) Describe the costs and benefits of a pricing skimming strategy to a firm, such as *T in the Bag*.   *2 marks*

4. Explain the benefits Alistair realised could be gained from segmenting the market.   *4 marks*

25 marks

Marketing:
T in the Bag

Case Study 3

Alistair, Shazia and Suzy sat nervously in the Head Office reception of a large sports retailer. Their quirky t-shirt, *T in the Bag*, inspired by the festival T in the Park, had caught the eye of a director, who was keen to sell the t-shirt in their UK shops, but wanted first to know more about their marketing plans.

As manager of promotion, Alistair explained they had lacked the finances to organise a TV campaign and instead had advertised on the social networking sites. Adverts in this medium were cheaper and allowed for better targeting of their audience. Also, colour and moving imagery gave impact to their products and ads could be easily changed to suit the season. Festival brochures, that were often retained as momentos of concerts, could also be used as an advertising medium.

When asked about their into the pipeline promotions, Shazia showed their range of point of sale materials, e.g. a display board showing a reveller wearing their t-shirt. She also offered the retailer a "sale or return" arrangement where any unsold t-shirts could be returned to reimburse any unsold stock. Shazia had also introduced a competition where the sports retail outlet with the highest t-shirt sales could win tickets to a music festival of their choice.

In return Suzy asked for support with direct selling. Customers could purchase their t-shirts directly from the sports retailers catalogue and website. Despite savings with fewer staff and high street outlets, the sports retailer was reluctant to sell in this way as they had experienced problems chasing in unpaid bills from students whose addresses frequently changed.

The director gave advice on distribution of the t-shirts. Selling via the sports shops would escalate sales, meaning *T in the Bag* should change to a Chinese manufacturer. The t-shirts could be delivered to an independent wholesaler who would package the products and organise deliveries to the sports retailer's shops. Image of the product was the primary consideration, so the t-shirt would initially be available in the shops before being put on sale via the catalogues. The director also added he would like the brand to act as a sponsor for the Commonwealth Games to get it associated with a healthy lifestyle and obtain increased exposure from re-runs of events on TV.

Questions

Write your ideas about each question in note form on the lines provided. You should then write out your full answers to this Case Study on a fresh piece of paper.

1. Discuss 4 advertising mediums that a firm, such as *T in the Bag,* could have used to promote its products.   *8 marks*

2. (a) Describe the term "into the pipeline promotions".   *1 mark*

   (b) Describe 4 ways in which a firm, such as *T in the Bag,* could encourage a wholesaler or retailer to stock their products.   *4 marks*

3. Describe 2 forms of direct selling a firm, such as *T in the Bag,* could use to maximise its sales.   *4 marks*

4. (a) Describe 2 factors that would influence a firm's, choice of channel of distribution.   *2 marks*

   (b) Describe the role of a wholesaler.   *4 marks*

5. Explain 2 benefits to a firm, such as *T in the Bag,* from sponsoring a major sporting event.   *2 marks*

25 marks

Operations:
Pizz-A-Fun

Case Study 1

A young couple, Ann-Marie and Paul, purchased a loss-making pizza factory from an old family friend and went about overhauling the whole operations process.

Ann-Marie's first task was to appoint a purchasing manager to reduce their list of suppliers from 40 to 10 and find a replacement for the existing unreliable supplier of cheese. The new supplier would be judged on the quality of the cheese, their prices (including opportunities for discounts) and the supplier's reliability in terms of deliveries and ICT compatibility.

Paul turned his attention to the factory layout. He carefully rearranged the production lines to allow for the easy delivery of the ingredients from the cold storerooms. The end of the production lines led into the packaging areas where the pizzas were individually wrapped and then passed into the loading bay.

Stock control would be important to the firm. Recent increases in stock had resulted in some ingredients going out of date, with suspicions that staff had been helping themselves to packets of cheese. This money could be used in advertising the firm and so was not to be wasted. Having too little stock would be expensive for the firm as bulk buying discounts would be lost for the small amount ordered. Staff would also be idle as the factory waited on the stocks levels to increase.

In response to this dilemma, Ann-Marie installed a computerised stock control system that allowed the raw material stocks to be controlled by actual pizzas sales. When the stocks fell below a certain amount, an order was automatically raised and sent via an "edi" link to the firm's supplier. This system responded to actual demand, avoiding human error and postal delays.

Currently, Paul was attending an operations course which explained the benefits of using a JIT system for delivery of large volume stock. Deliveries of the pureed tomatoes would be stored at the supplier and delivered to the factory just in time for it to be used on the production line. This would free up storage space at the factory for another pizza production line which could increase sales and profits. Paul, however, was concerned that quality checks would be passed on to the supplier, more frequent deliveries would be needed which could increase costs and that the pizza factory would be vulnerable to unexpected large orders that couldn't be met by the supplier at such short notice.

Questions

Write your ideas about each question in note form on the lines provided. You should then write out your full answers to this Case Study on a fresh piece of paper.

1. Under the heading of Operations, identify the problems the pizza
   factory was experiencing.   *4 marks*

2. Describe the criteria by which a firm could assess their supplier.   *5 marks*

3. (a) Describe to Ann-Marie and Paul the problems of having too much
       stock.   *4 marks*

   (b) Describe to Ann-Marie and Paul the problems of having too little
       stock.   *4 marks*

4. (a) Describe the concept of "just in time" stock management.   *2 marks*

   (b) Explain to Ann-Marie and Paul the costs and benefits of using this
       system.   *6 marks*

                                                                    25 marks

Operations:
Pizz-A-Fun

Case Study 2

The overhaul of the pizza factory for Ann-Marie and Paul was a learning exercise on the methods of production.

The majority of production lines would follow a batch method of production. A group of pizzas would be made with certain ingredients and then the lines would be stopped, cleaned down and another group would be made with different toppings. The turkey and sausage was popular at Christmas whilst ham and pineapple pizzas saw their highest sales over the summer months. Ann-Marie could bulk buy certain ingredients such as ham and the output and quality of each batch of pizzas would improve as the workers gained experience and minimised mistakes.

On a rare occasion Paul would produce a one-off, party pizza for corporate clients, made exactly to their specifications, i.e. their choice of ingredients. It was so large in size, the head of the bakery section took charge of making it and delivered it by hand in a specially designed box. It was time-consuming and sales were lost in the production of pizzas but it secured a premium price and often gave the company some free publicity in their client's newsletter.

A recent order by a large supermarket gave Paul the idea to introduce a flow method of production with the cheese and tomato pizza. It would need large financial investment in robotic equipment, also careful scheduling of the staff and output, with production running 24 hours a day over a set period. The supermarket demanded dedicated staff be put on their account, but promised opportunities for bulk buying discounts and large sales and profit.

The transport was arranged around the client. Analysis of the database of clients showed the supermarket accounted for 60 % of their turnover and so pizzas deliveries to their warehouse were transported in a specially air-conditioned lorry with a satellite navigation system to track movement of stock around the country. The smaller, local businesses, such as chip shops and restaurants would have their deliveries in smaller vans with the *Pizz-A-Fun* signage on the side. The money made from the supermarkets helped pay for deliveries by plane to several clients in the Outer Hebrides. The speed of delivery allowed them to maximise the shelf life and minimise handling of the food.

Questions

Write your ideas about each question in note form on the lines provided. You should then write out your full answers to this Case Study on a fresh piece of paper.

1. Describe to Ann-Marie the advantages of using a batch method of production. *4 marks*

2. Describe to Ann-Marie the disadvantages of using a job method of production. *4 marks*

3. Describe to Ann-Marie the advantages and disadvantages of using a flow method of production. *6 marks*

4. Identify an example of a product, other than pizzas, for each of the methods of production mentioned. *3 marks*

5. Describe the factors Ann-Marie and Paul would have considered when deciding on a suitable method of transport for their pizzas. *5 marks*

6. Describe 2 forms of ICT that would have helped Paul to manage the supermarket. *2 marks*

7. Explain the advantage of having signage (brand name) on the side of the pizza delivery vans. *1 mark*

25 marks

Operations:
Pizz-A-Fun

Case Study 3

A short telephone survey of their main customers showed to Ann-Marie and Paul that quality was a major factor when selecting a supplier of pizzas. This became one of *Pizz-A-Fun*'s main objectives.

Paul, initially, benchmarked his pizzas against the industry leader. He bought a full range of their competitor's pizzas and back at his factory laid them out on the bakery tables. He spent the next three days analysing each part of the pizza, its thickness, the amount of tomato and cheese used, the style of the packaging, price and so on. This allowed him to set the standard of quality by which the *Pizz-A-Fun* products would be measured.

Paul then introduced quality checks at key stages on the production lines. Twice a day, for example, the dough would be checked for its consistency and the tomatoes for their flavour. The supplier's delivery vans of the raw materials were checked and so too their quality of raw materials. Any equipment purchased has to meet the industry guidelines and have a CE standard to ensure they had met European standards. This form of quality assurance gave Paul peace of mind that each stage in the supply chain would of a quality standard.

In addition, a pizza from every customer's batch was checked just prior to delivery as a final confirmation that no problems had occurred, known as quality control. Paul noticed that after two months customer complaints had reduced and also the number of pizzas being returned. This improved their reputation and saved money in paperwork and accounting for damaged stock.

Ann-Marie suggested quality should also be a matter for their workforce. Every month a group of around five staff met at the end of their production line and discussed matters that were affecting their work. Angelica was appointed to head up these quality circles so staff could be more open without fear of offending the owners. Angelica received training and ensured all suggestions were fully addressed. At first, staff simply raised complaints but gradually some enterprising solutions were given which compensated for any lost production. The supervisors, for example, wanted to come off the hourly rate of pay and instead move to a salary. They would have to work longer hours but projects would be given more time and be completed to a higher standard.

Questions

Write your ideas about each question in note form on the lines provided. You should then write out your full answers to this Case Study on a fresh piece of paper.

1. Describe 4 methods of improving quality for a firm such as *Pizz-A-Fun*.   *4 marks*

2. Explain the costs and benefits of using quality circles in a firm such as *Pizz-A-Fun*.   *6 marks*

3. Describe to Ann-Marie and Paul ways in which "total quality management" could be introduced to improve the overall quality in the factory.   *2 marks*

4. Explain the benefits of improved quality to:
   - a firm
   - a customer   *4 marks*

5. "Hourly rate" and "piece rate" are 2 methods of payment.

   (a) Describe both these payment systems.   *2 marks*

   (b) Describe 3 other methods of payment the firm could use.   *3 marks*

6. "To improve quality" was an objective of the factory right from the beginning of their trading.

   (a) Describe what type of **objective** this was.   *2 marks*

   (b) Describe 2 tactical decisions Ann-Marie and Paul could make to achieve this objective.   *2 marks*

                                                                    25 marks

Financial Management: 2Fit Gym

Case Study 1

2Fit Gym was started up by Bob Show but, after only five years, he was thinking of selling up. Gym membership had fallen, poor record keeping meant chasing unpaid bills was difficult and the bank had refused to grant him another loan.

Bob had been reluctant to learn much about the main accounting documents. The trading and profit and loss accounts show his gross profit is steady, yet his overall net profit is low. The bank manager has advised him to reduce his cost of goods sold by seeking out a cheaper supplier of his gym equipment and reduce his expenses by lowering wages and banning overtime.

His balance sheet shows he has a far greater number of current liabilities than current assets which leaves him with a poor working capital. The bank manager advises this would be resolved if he increased the price of his gym membership or ensured stock such as shampoo and towels were not being stolen by staff.

His bank manager had identified many problems with his cash flow. Currently he gives no attention to chasing unpaid bills. These problems would be solved, he is advised, if he offered incentives such as discounts for early payment or encouraged customers to pay by direct debit. He has been spending too much of the daily drawings on entertaining friends and family. His sales are also low, possibly due to poor pricing strategies and the fact that his gym equipment has been purchased rather than leased. If he had leased the equipment, breakdowns would be covered by the leasing firm and modern updates could be quickly arranged. He had borrowed his loans at a high rate of interest which meant there has never been much retained profit left to reinvest in the gym.

Bob has decided to take a crash course in accounts and has given himself one year to turn the fortunes of the business round.

Questions

Write your ideas about each question in note form on the lines provided. You should then write out your full answers to this Case Study on a fresh piece of paper.

1. Under the heading "finance", identify the problems *2Fit Gym* was experiencing before Bob Show took a closer interest in his accounts.   *3 marks*

2. (a) Describe 5 cash flow problems a firm, such as *2Fit Gym*, could face with its finances.   *5 marks*

    (b) Describe 5 ways in which a firm, such as *2Fit Gym*, could resolve these cash flow problems.   *5 marks*

3. Describe the following terms:
    * working capital
    * creditors
    * current assets
    * current liabilities   *4 marks*

4. Describe 2 factors that could cause a firm's gross profit to fall.   *2 marks*

5. Describe how a manager, such as Bob Show, could improve his net profit.   *3 marks*

6. Describe 3 ways in which *2Fit Gym* could improve its working capital.   *3 marks*

25 marks

Financial Management:
2Fit Gym

Case Study 2

Bob Show, owner of *2Fit Gym*, was facing bankruptcy and had enrolled himself onto an accounting course and quickly learned how to perform accounting ratios.

To improve his gross profit ratio he attempted to increase prices. This was introduced in the New Year when demand for the gym was high. To support this decision and improve his net profit margin he changed his expensive TV ad to a cheaper direct mail campaign using his database of addresses and by popping leaflets into the two local papers. He negotiated a cheaper lease with his weight-lifting equipment and, as a result, his mark-up ratio also improved. He was able to monitor how successful these actions were through the return on capital ratios. He frequently calculated the return *2Fit Gym* was giving on the money he'd invested against the return a bank would have offered.

Bob was fully prepared when asked by his bank manager as to how he intended to improve his current ratios i.e. his ability to improve his short term debts. Bob had planned to increase his current assets by encouraging every new member to pay by monthly direct debit and so the cash in his bank was boosted. Imposing a minimum yearly membership increased the number of debtors. He also hired a part time accounts clerk who organised his unpaid bills and gradually reduced his current liabilities. His concerns were confirmed when he calculated his acid test ratio and an answer of 0.5:1 was found. His stock of gym clothing, a poor seller and not guaranteed to sell, was tying up his money and lowering his ability to pay his debts in a crisis.

Bob, ever the canny businessman, realised that these ratios could not tell the full story. Declining gym membership could be the result of a looming recession. All his calculations were last year's figures and initiatives such as the dance classes were not being individually assessed in these ratios. Comparisons with a large chain of gyms were pointless and the accounts were hiding the current problems.

Questions

Write your ideas about each question in note form on the lines provided. You should then write out your full answers to this Case Study on a fresh piece of paper.

1. Describe the reasons why a firm, such as *2Fit Gym*, would be interested in accounting ratios.   *4 marks*

2. (a) Describe 3 profitability ratios a firm, such as *2Fit Gym*, would be interested in to achieve a better understanding of their business.   *6 marks*

    (b) Explain how a firm, such as *2Fit Gym*, could improve each of the ratios mentioned in 2 (a).   *4 marks*

3. (a) Describe 2 liquidity ratios a firm, such as *2Fit Gym*, would be interested in to achieve a better understanding of their business.   *4 marks*

    (b) Explain how a firm, such as *2Fit Gym*, could improve each of the ratios mentioned in 3 (a).   *2 marks*

4. Explain the limitations of relying solely on accounting ratios.   *5 marks*

25 marks

Financial Management:
2Fit Gym

Case Study 3

Bob Show, owner of *2Fit Gym*, despite facing bankruptcy last year, had turned the business round after gaining a better understanding of his accounts. He was now keen to forecast his income (receipts) and payments for the coming year and his bank manager had advised drawing up a cash flow forecast (budget).

Initially doubtful, Bob was converted when he realised the benefits of planning when his bank balance would appear in the negative. An extension to his bank overdraft could be promptly arranged and with the early warning, win favour with his bank manager. He could plan when to expand the sauna facilities i.e. during a period when surplus cash was forecast. The forecast also predicted a quieter time over the summer months and therefore a good time to renovate the café. With this planned increase in spending, Bob decided to cut back on staff hours. His forecasting ability was first challenged when his projected figures were very different from his actual ones, but gradually improved as he became better at reading his market.

Bob was thankful he had a better grasp of finances when his accounts attracted some attention following his decision to sell shares in the gym. He was able to talk potential shareholders through documents such as his cash flow statement and explain convincingly all movements of cash in and out of the business in the past year. In addition, when he appointed two new managers, they had consulted his accounts to gauge an appropriate wage level. He was able to improve relations with the Inland Revenue by submitting, on time, his tax returns and avoid a fine as in previous years. He secured a lease of £1million worth of gym equipment when the supplier could easily calculate his liquidity and, finally, at a meeting with the local community, obtained planning permission for an extension to his gym on the financial strength of his business.

Bob smiled at his new mission statement: slim figures in the gym mirrors, fat figures in the company books.

Questions

Write your ideas about each question in note form on the lines provided. You should then write out your full answers to this Case Study on a fresh piece of paper.

1. (a) Describe the term cash flow forecast (budget).   *2 marks*

    (b) Describe reasons why a firm would draw up a cash flow forecast.   *5 marks*

2. Describe the term cash flow statement.   *2 marks*

3. Describe the interest 5 stakeholders would have in the accounts of a firm, such as *2Fit Gym*.   *5 marks*

4. Explain why a firm, such as *2Fit Gym*, can appear profitable but still have cash flow problems.   *2 marks*

5. Discuss 3 sources of finance a firm, such as *2Fit Gym*, could access to help with the building of their multi-million pound extension.   *6 marks*

6. Describe the responsibilities an owner, such as Bob Show, would put into a job description for a new accountant.   *3 marks*

25 marks

Human Resource Management: **Bootus**

Case Study 1

Several years ago George went for a job interview with a local firm distributing computer games for Microsoft. The manager had spoken to him over the phone to invite him for an interview the next day. George had no time either to prepare his CV or get a reference from his previous employer. His interview lasted five minutes where the manager did most of the talking. He wasn't informed that he was successful until a month later by which time he had already accepted a better job working for *Bootus*, a manufacturer of fur-lined boots, organising its logistics i.e. arranging all the deliveries of stock to the customers.

Bootus was expanding and a job vacancy had come up in logistics. The post was then analysed to establish if it could be justified financially. The HR Director took charge of compiling a job description to clarify the tasks and duties of the post and then she wrote out a person specification where the desired experience, qualifications and personality of the new recruit were confirmed.

Bootus had advertised in the *Herald* newspaper and, based on his application form, invited George for an interview along with 10 other candidates. He had been asked to give a presentation on his ideas for improving the logistics of the firm. He sat a numerical test to compare him with the other applicants and a medical test as aspects of the job were very physical. He made a good impression and was invited back for a second interview where he met the rest of the staff and had a more in-depth chat with the Managing Director.

He was informed on the evening of the second interview of his success with his application. He is now Logistics Director and has contributed to expanding *Bootus* to manufacture and distribute boots for the whole of the UK.

Questions

Write your ideas about each question in note form on the lines provided. You should then write out your full answers to this Case Study on a fresh piece of paper.

1. Under the heading, "Human Resources", identify 3 problems with the first company's approach to selection. *3 marks*

2. Describe the recruitment process a firm, such as *Bootus*, could use to ensure it gets the right candidate for the job. *5 marks*

3. Describe a selection process a firm, such as *Bootus*, could use to ensure it gets the right candidate for the job. *5 marks*

4. Describe 4 methods of testing a firm, such as *Bootus*, could use to help with their selection of a suitable candidate. *8 marks*

5. Describe the advantages and disadvantages to *Bootus* of advertising their job in a national newspaper. *4 marks*

25 marks

Human Resource Management: **Bootus**

Case Study 2

On arrival at his new firm, *Bootus*, manufacturers and distributors of fur lined boots, George initially underwent some induction training. He went on a tour of the factory and was introduced to his line manager, Rachel. He received some basic health and safety training and was shown the company manual to read up on the firm's procedures, such as how to handle disciplinary matters.

In the early months George received some "on the job" training. George shadowed Rachel as she showed him how to process customers' orders via the computer system. She listened in to telephone calls as George negotiated deliveries with customers and coached him on how to be firm with an outstanding query without losing favour with the customer.

As George became more experienced he started to take on more "off the job" training such as an ICT logistics course at the local college to coincide with the introduction of a new ICT system at *Bootus*. It was expensive and some deliveries suffered in George's absence but his expertise improved and so too his commitment when he volunteered to come in over weekends just to catch up. He was allowed to visit a sister firm with a similar logistics system and attended a conference where he networked with other logistics managers.

His department expanded and he introduced appraisals of staff to ensure standards improved. He set individualised targets for each worker and identified their training needs to help achievement of these goals. Morale was raised when workers received good feedback and George had better control of output levels. Changes became easier to introduce as staff had been consulted beforehand and George felt quietly proud at the end of a staff "paintballing" activity, when they gave him a card that read, "you're a bad hit with the paint but a big hit with us".

Questions

Write your ideas about each question in note form on the lines provided. You should then write out your full answers to this Case Study on a fresh piece of paper.

1. Describe an induction programme a firm, such as *Bootus*, could give to a new member of staff. *4 marks*

2. (a) Describe the terms "on the job and "off the job" training"? *2 marks*

   (b) Describe 3 methods of "on the job" training a firm, such as *Bootus*, could give to an employee such as George. *3 marks*

   (c) Describe 3 methods of "off the job" training a firm, such as *Bootus*, could give to an employee. *3 marks*

3. Explain the potential costs and benefits to a firm, such as *Bootus*, from training your staff. *6 marks*

4. (a) Define the term appraisal system. *1 mark*

   (b) Explain the benefits of an appraisal system to a firm, such as *Bootus*. *3 marks*

5. Describe 2 non-financial ways a firm, such as *Bootus*, could motivate their staff. *3 marks*

25 marks

Human Resource Management: **Bootus**

Case Study 3

In the early years of trading, *Bootus*, a manufacturing firm of fur lined boots, had experienced industrial relations problems with its staff. Due to sit-ins and strikes in the past, the owners had refused to invite the unions into any negotiations regarding pay and conditions. There was a lot of resentment, many staff left and those who stayed were unwilling to accept any changes to work practices such as the introduction of new technology on production lines.

Under new management, *Bootus* made improving staff relations a priority. They listened to staff opinions via quality circles and negotiated changes with staff rather than just passing out instructions at staff meetings. When changing suppliers, for instance, the managers would consult staff for their opinions and when a dispute arose over wage levels amongst the males and females, *Bootus* invited ACAS to arbitrate.

At staff meetings, *Bootus* outlined the procedure for seeking assistance with any industrial problems. A worker was encouraged to first speak to their boss and if the problem continued then staff could approach the HR department or their union rep. Staff were also shown the ACAS website which offered advice on a full range of industrial problems. In accordance with the *Health and Safety at Work Act 1974* and, in addition to *Bootus'* duties of care, staff were told of their responsibilities such as wearing safety glasses on the production line. *Bootus* rewrote their job adverts in line with the guidelines in the *Sex Discrimination Act*, and requests for absences to acknowledge religious festivals were checked via the *Employment Equality (Religion or Belief) Regulations 2003*. *Bootus* ensured they avoided any potential legal claims which also protected their reputation.

Overall, *Bootus*'s open style of management allowed staff to feel like valued stakeholders in the firm. Staff absenteeism fell and with changes being easier to introduce the firm became very responsive to customers needs and sales and profits rose.

Questions

Write your ideas about each question in note form on the lines provided. You should then write out your full answers to this Case Study on a fresh piece of paper.

1. Under the heading of "Human Resources", identify the problems *Bootus* was facing in the early years. *4 marks*

2. Describe 4 forms of industrial action staff could take against a firm, such as *Bootus*. *4 marks*

3. Describe the measures a firm, such as *Bootus*, could introduce to improve employee relations between managers and staff. *5 marks*

4. Describe the steps an employee would go through if they felt they disagreed with action taken by a firm, such as *Bootus*. *5 marks*

5. Describe 4 forms of legislation a firm would follow to ensure it was protecting its workers rights. *4 marks*

6. Explain 3 effects on a firm, such as *Bootus*, of poor staff relations. *3 marks*

25 marks

NAB 1: Business in Contemporary Society
ChocOBloc

Case Study 1

Who would have thought a gorilla playing the drums would boost the sales of a chocolate company?

The directors of the chocolate company, *Tartan Chocs Ltd*, had a rude wake-up call when, thanks to a performing gorilla, a competitor's sales soared. Their results had, however, plummetted in the last year. The directors: Hannah, Lewis and Sarah, held some crisis talks and set about gathering information and researching strategies that could turn around the fortunes of the business.

Lewis was tasked to undertake a SWOT analysis. This gave him a current picture of their business and helped to identify such things as strengths that could be exploited and threats that had to be anticipated. He attached this information to an email and sent to the other directors.

Hannah had consulted a Mintel report that broke down into age range the consumption figures for chocolate across the UK. It was clear the age group 14–21 had the highest numbers and so Hannah suggested they consider this group as their target audience. She also checked the sales team's figures and spotted areas of Scotland where sales were poor and staff were potentially wasting their time, such as the tourist shops. Wandering round supermarkets, she observed the leading competitors brand and noted their strategies such as product range, packaging and pricing. Finally, using their database of clients, Hannah phoned round and obtained some honest opinions from small newsagents as to their current opinion of their chocolate bar.

Sarah took all of this information and, via a conference call, presented to the other directors, Hannah's findings. She sent a spreadsheet showing the break down of sales by region and the proposed areas of the country the company should target. Based on the Mintel figures, she confirmed their target market and was able to forecast sales for the coming year. Catherine, their ICT manager, had even used a CAD system to design some ideas for packaging that the directors were sent and invited to change and comment on.

After a month of intensive meetings, the directors finally took the decision to focus over the next five years on increasing sales by 5% per year. They would adopt Sarah's recommendations and use the steps of a decision-making model to enable them to logically think through the problem and come up with several alternatives as to how this objective could be achieved.

Top of the list was to change the name, and thanks to Catherine, the name *ChocOBloc* was formed.

Write your ideas about each question in note form on the lines provided. You should then write out your full answers to this NAB on a fresh piece of paper.

1. (a) Name the type of business described in the passage.   *1 mark*

    (b) Describe the characteristics of the different types of organisation using the criteria of ownership, control and finance.   *6 marks*

2. (a) From the passage, identify one strategic and one tactical decision that *Tartan Choc Ltd* has made. Justify your choices.   *4 marks*

    (b) Explain how the objectives of *Tartan Toffee* may have changed over the past year.   *2 marks*

3. Before deciding on their new goal for the business, *Tartan Chocs Ltd* made use of several decision-making tools. Discuss the advantages and disadvantages of using structured decision-making models when making a decision.   *6 marks*

4. In order to support their decisions, *Tartan Chocs Ltd* used a variety of different sources of information. From the text, identify examples of sources of information and describe their reliability and value.   *6 marks*

5. (a) Explain how *Tartan Chocs Ltd* made use of 2 different types of ICT.   *4 marks*

    (b) Describe the costs and benefits of using these types of ICT for *Tartan Chocs Ltd*.   *6 marks*

6. Explain the influences of *Tartan Choc Ltd*'s stakeholders on the objectives of the organisation.   *5 marks*

40 marks

NAB 2: Marketing and Operations
ChocOBloc

Case Study 2

ChocOBloc was the newly formed brand of the struggling company, *Tartan Chocs Ltd*. To assist with the launch of their new brand they had recruited the services of a marketing consultant who had submitted the following marketing strategy:

- Alter the packaging to show brighter colours.
- Aim to sell the product in retail outlets visisted by the target audience of 14–21 year olds, such as *Topshop*.
- Launch an advertising campaign using radio to get the brand name known first, supported later with billboards near universities and schools.
- The price was to be kept in line with the leading competitor's brand of chocolate.

These recommendations had been based on an internet survey of 400 students. The consultant had also undertaken more in-depth interviews using different flavours of chocolate and trialled these with the target audience. Each reaction was noted for later analysis. The costing of the ad campaigns had been collected from the quotes given by the various radio stations and billboard companies.

ChocOBloc's operations would have to be changed to meet the demands of this new marketing strategy. To cope with the increase in demand *ChocOBloc* would need to change several of their suppliers and Lewis, one of the directors, is keen to introduce new quality initiatives to raise the standard of the chocolate in line with the new image of the brand. A few trial-run quality circles have already proved successful in raising staff morale but Lewis still has lessons to learn in managing the group suggestions.

ChocOBloc currently uses a batch method of production which allows for different flavours and different sizes of chocolate bar. Lewis believes a few contracts with the large supermarkets could see the possibility of a flow method of production.

The company is also considering changing their vans for new air conditioned models with the eye-catching signage on the side. Lewis was also keen to take advantage of the cheaper price of vans during the credit crunch.

Write your ideas about each question in note form on the lines provided. You should then write out your full answers to this NAB on a fresh piece of paper.

1. Explain why each of the elements of the marketing mix had to be altered to improve *ChocOBloc*'s chances of success.   *4 marks*

2. After altering the brand name to *ChocOBloc*, explain the effect this will have on the other elements of the marketing mix.   *2 marks*

3. (a) Describe and justify 2 ways in which Tartan Chocs Ltd could segment its market.   *4 marks*

   (b) Explain how market segmentation can help a firm.   *4 marks*

4. Market research is vital to an organisation such as *Tartan Chocs Ltd*.

   (a) Describe 2 ways of carrying out field research.   *2 marks*

   (b) Explain the advantages of field research over desk research.   *4 marks*

5. *Tartan Chocs Ltd* will have to changes its supplier to cope with the anticipated increase in demand. Explain the factors which may have to be taken into consideration when *Tartan Chocs Ltd* selects a supplier.   *4 marks*

6. (a) Describe and justify the production method used by *Tartan Chocs Ltd* to produce its chocolate bar.   *2 marks*

   (b) Discuss the advantages of the production method suggested in 6 (a) over another production method *Tartan Chocs Ltd* could have chosen.   *4 marks*

7. (a) Explain why quality is important to a firm such as *Tartan Chocs Ltd*.   *3 marks*

   (b) Describe the costs involved in introducing a quality system.   *4 marks*

8. Explain the factors *Tartan Chocs Ltd* would have to take into consideration when deciding on the most efficient delivery system for the firm.   *3 marks*

40 marks

NAB 3: Finance and Operations
ChocOBloc

Case Study 3

Hannah, Lewis and Sarah, directors of *Tartan Chocs Ltd*, sat in the boardroom to listen to a presentation by the Accounts department on the previous year's financial performance of their new brand of chocolate, called *ChocOBloc*. These results would significantly influence the future direction of the business.

The following ratios were shown:

Ratio	Last Year	This Year
Gross profit as % of sales	18%	25%
Net profit as % of sales	12%	8%
Return on capital employed	17%	22%
Current ratio	1.3:1	2.1:1
Acid test ratio	1.5:1	0.5:1

Some ratios looked favourable whilst others raised some concerns. Hannah explained that a successful advertising campaign had helped them exceed their sales targets and changing suppliers had resulted in a healthy gross profit. However, expenses had risen considerably and Sarah drew attention to the build up of stock.

Lewis suggested drawing up budgets for each department to keep a better control of costs and avoid unfavourable performance.

Hannah agreed and took the opportunity to highlight the increase in sales as a need for Human Resources to appoint a new sales manager to control the expanding market. This would involve a thorough recruitment and selection process to ensure the best candidates applied for the post.

Improvements to their stock handling would require an updating of their computerised stock control equipment which Sarah advised would require training for all staff involved. Some external courses could be given to key personnel and then cascaded down to the other members of staff through shadowing sessions.

Lewis suggested all staff receive a refresher course on the basic conditions of the *Health and Safety at Work Act* to protect the firm's insurance.

Write your ideas about each question in note form on the lines provided. You should then write out your full answers to this NAB on a fresh piece of paper.

1. Explain the role and importance of the finance function for a firm such as *Tartan Chocs Ltd.*   *3 marks*

2. (a) From the figures provided, discuss the changes in performance of a profitability and liquidity ratio over the two years.   *4 marks*

   (b) Discuss actions that *Tartan Chocs Ltd* could take to improve the performance of any of the ratios mentioned.   *4 marks*

3. Discuss the limitations of ratios for a firm such as *Tartan Chocs Ltd.*   *4 marks*

4. Describe the benefits of using budgets to help monitor and control the performance of a business.   *4 marks*

5. Explain the role of the Human Resources department in helping a firm such as *Tartan Chocs Ltd* achieve their objectives.   *4 marks*

6. (a) Describe an effective recruitment and selection process for *Tartan Chocs Ltd.*   *4 marks*

   (b) Explain why an effective selection process is essential for a firm such as *Tartan Chocs Ltd.*   *3 marks*

7. Describe 3 benefits of training for each of the following:
   - employee
   - employer   *6 marks*

8. Describe how 2 pieces of employment legislation could affect the running of *Tartan Chocs Ltd.*   *4 marks*

40 marks

Vocabulary Tests

The following terms have been randomly selected from each Unit. Test yourself as to their meaning then check your responses against the Answers at the end of the textbook.

Note: if you struggle with any terms then mark an * against it and, next time you're revising, you'll know which areas were your weakest.

Unit 1 Business in Contemporary Society

Limited liability _____

_____

Tertiary Sector _____

_____

Publicly funded organisation _____

_____

Economies of scale_____

_____

Entrepreneur _____

_____

Franchisee _____

_____

Hire Purchase _____

_____

Debentures _____

_____

Diversification _____

_____

Outsourcing _____

_____

Continued →

Unit 1 Business in Contemporary Society *continued*

Management buy-in _____

_____

SME _____

_____

Unit 2 Business Information & ICT

Quantitative information _____

_____

Qualitative information _____

_____

E-commerce _____

_____

CAD _____

_____

Sources of information _____

_____

Types of information _____

_____

Unit 3 Decision-making in Business

Strategic decision _____

_____

Tactical decision _____

_____

SWOT analysis _____

_____

POGADSCIE _____

_____

Unit 4 Internal Organisation

Functional grouping _____

_____

Chain of command _____

_____

Span of control _____

_____

Line manager _____

_____

Hierarchy _____

_____

Formal organisation structure _____

_____

Informal organisation structure _____

_____

Entrepreneurial structure _____

_____

Matrix _____

_____

Decentralised _____

_____

Delayering _____

_____

Downsizing _____

_____

Empowerment _____

_____

Corporate culture _____

_____

Unit 5 Marketing

Product orientation _____

_____

Market segmentation _____

_____

Niche market _____

_____

Undifferentiated marketing _____

_____

Consumer audit _____

_____

Hall test _____

_____

Random stratified sampling _____

_____

Product line extension _____

_____

Loss leaders _____

_____

Direct selling _____

_____

In to the pipeline promotions _____

_____

Unit 6 Operations

System design _____

_____

Purchasing mix _____

_____

Computerised stock control system _____

_____

JIT _____

_____

Commission _____

_____

Capital intensive production _____

_____

Benchmarking _____

_____

Quality assurance _____

_____

BSI _____

_____

Distribution mix _____

_____

Unit 7 Financial Management

Gross profit _____

_____

Net profit _____

_____

Fixed asset _____

_____

Current liability _____

_____

Debtors _____

_____

Creditors _____

_____

Working capital _____

_____

Drawings _____

_____

Liquidity _____

_____

Net profit margin _____

_____

Acid test ratio _____

_____

Cash flow budget _____

_____

Unit 8 Human Resource Management

Job description _____

_____

Person specification _____

_____

Aptitude test_____

_____

Induction training _____

_____

Off the job training _____

_____

Job rotation_____

_____

Appraisal _____

_____

Arbitration _____

_____

Go slow _____

_____

Exam Tips

1. Note when the question is asking about the **customer** and when it's asking about the **firm**.

    Example
    Describe the advantages of the internet to the **firm**.

2. Avoid repetitions or flip arguments.

    Example
    Primary information is **cheap.**
    Secondary information is **expensive.**

    This will only receive one mark as it is a repeat of the same cost argument.

3. Note that when questions require an explanation, your answer needs two parts to the answer.

    Example
    Explain the internal factors that could hold back a firm's expansion.

    Answer
    A firm may lack experienced managers (identification part) who are unable to use the appropriate decision-making models to handle the decisions necessary for growth (explanation part).

    Only when these two parts are present does the sentence get a mark.

4. Note the word **justify**, which asks for an advantage but NOT a disadvantage.

    Example
    Describe and **justify** a source of finance for a small business that is just starting out.

    Answer
    The firm could access a government grant which is a lump sum of money given by the government to the firm often in an area of high unemployment (describe part). This is given by the government as the firm will be creating jobs which benefits the government in terms of taxes and saves the government money in terms of social security payments (justify part).

5. When asked to describe the **conflict** of two stakeholders, both conflicts have to be described to get **one** mark.

    Example
    The customer wants the firm's products to be priced cheaply with good quality, whilst the manager wants high prices and is prepared to sacrifice quality. (1 mark)

6. Be aware of trick questions.

    Example
    Other than a mortgage what 2 forms of long term finance could a firm access?

    Note – don't mention a mortgage.

Answers

Remember: these answers provide a summary of the main points that a marker would be looking for, they are not exhaustive.

Coffee & Chords: Case Study 1

1 • a recession was looming
 • supplier's food prices were too high
 • deliveries were often late to the café
 • the supplier's invoicing system was giving the firm problems
 • cash flow

3 marks

2 • a partnership does not sell shares in the firm as a means of finance, a limited company will sell shares but only to friends and family
 • the partners of a firm will have unlimited liability which means they are responsible for all of the debts whereas the shareholders of a limited company will have limited liability where they only stand to lose the value of their shares
 • the limited company has to produce more legal documents such as Memorandum of Association and Articles of Association when starting out whereas a partnership is liable to produce the Partnership Agreement
 • the partnership is limited to 20 partners whereas the limited company's shareholders can exceed this limit

4 marks

3 (a) • owners savings – which are the funds supplied by the owner (in case of a limited company, by the shareholder) these funds do not attract interest payments like a bank loan and it allows the owner to retain control of their business without having to sell shares

 • grant – from the Prince's Trust awarded to young people to assist them with the risk in setting up a firm, these funds do not have to be paid back
 • leasing – this involves renting equipment or property for an agreed period of time from another firm without eventually taking ownership, this allows the firm to spread their repayments and avoid a high initial investment at a time when they have little spare cash
 • hire purchase – a firm will rent equipment from another firm a for an agreed period of time to be repaid in instalments until the last payment when the renting firm takes ownership of the equipment, this allows the firm to earn money whilst it is paying back the price of the equipment. At the end of the payment period the firm has an asset it can sell on at the end of its life

6 marks

(b) • Scottish Enterprise – provide advice on where to obtain funding, information on a number of issues such as legal advice and how to go about exporting your products
 • Careers Scotland – provide advice on how to recruit, select and train your staff
 • Local Authorities – provide advice on obtaining planning premission and locating premises

2 marks

64

4 An entrepreneur can have the following characteristics:
- they can spot a gap in the market AND will put this idea into practice
- they combine one or all of the factors of production, such as land, labour, capital and enterprise in order to manufacture the product or deliver the service
- they take the risks of the business being a failure or a success
- they make the strategic decisions in the firm associated with the marketing, operations and financing of the firm

4 marks

5 (a) Gianni wanted to grow using the backward vertical integration method.

1 mark

(b) Advantages:
- Gianni has a chance to control the quality of his supplies
- Gianni has a chance to improve on the reliability of the supplier's deliveries
- Gianni can cut the cost of the supplier's prices and absorb any profit from deliveries to other firms into his own business
- Gianni can standardise the paperwork and reduce the number of invoicing problems between the two businesses

Disadvantages:
- this is new area of business from the café and so it brings more risk simply than buying over another café
- there are not the same opportunities to achieve economies of scale as different products will be purchased for both firms
- Gianni and Chiara may spread themselves too thinly as they attempt to enter a new market

5 marks

Coffee & Chords: Case Study 2

1 (a) *Exam tip:* For any question with the word 'interest', simply think of what the stakeholder would 'want'.

- bank – would want *Coffee & Chords* to be in a position to pay their loan back within the agreed period of time
- local council – would want *Coffee & Chords* to abide by the law and to enhance the look of the neighbourhood
- suppliers – would want *Coffee & Chords* to pay their bills promptly and offer the firm a lot of repeat custom
- customers – would want quality goods at cheap prices
- workers – want job security and a fair wage
- managers – would want an opportunity for promotion

5 marks

(b) *Exam tip:* For any question with the word 'influence', simply think of what 'action' the stakeholder could make against the firm and the consequence of this action.
- bank – may refuse to grant *Coffee & Chords* a loan which means they have to go elseswhere for their funding
- local council – may refuse to grant *Coffee & Chords* planning permission which could hold back their expansion plans
- suppliers – may raise the price of their goods which will increase *Coffee & Chords* costs and potentially lower their profits
- customers – may feel *Coffee & Chords* are not providing a good service and so decide to go to their competitior's business
- workers – may feel the conditions are not acceptable at *Coffee & Chords* and so decide to take some industrial action such as a strike to let the management know how they feel
- managers – may make a decision that will affect how the business is run such as deciding to launch a new home delivery service

5 marks

2 *Exam tip*: it is better to mention the business and the local community in the one sentence in order to fully explain the conflict.
- the business may wish to open later whilst the local community may object to the noise levels
- the business may wish to decorate the shop front in a modern style which could be at odds with the local community's desire for a more traditional look
- the business may sell goods which are already on sale in other shops in the community, e.g. another café, and so other shops may object

3 marks

3 *Coffee & Chords* may have to:
- lower their prices or offer better deals to attract customers away from their competitors
- undertake more research to keep in touch with their customers and stay ahead of the competition
- take out copyright to prevent their ideas from being copied
- advertise to ensure they raise awareness of their name to customers
- accept a smaller market share and subsequent fall in sales targets

2 marks

4 (a) • survival – *Coffee & Chords* may seek to simply break even in their first year of trading
- sales maximisation – *Coffee & Chords* may, through promotional pricing techniques, aim to get as many sales as possible in order to bring a lively atmosphere to the café
- profit maximisation – *Coffee & Chords* could aim to obtain as many profits by offering expensive beers or charging for entry for the open mic nights
- growth – *Coffee & Chords* could aim to open many more cafés though the frachising route or to expand the range of food and drink they offer

- social responsibility – *Coffee & Chords* could make it a priority to look after the environment when undertaking their business through initiatives such as recycling or providing bins outside the café
- enhance their quality of service – *Coffee & Chords* could get a goal to improve the service they offer their customers by putting all their staff through training

3 marks

(b) *Note: it is not necessary to match your statements in this section exactly with the points made in the previous section.*
- check their sales records to spot if their sales are increasing
- put customer comment cards in the cafés to gauge if the quality of service is improving
- annual accounts can be checked to confirm if profits are rising at the desired rate
- Chiara and Gianni could conduct appraisals of staff to see if their objectives have been met
- Chiara and Gianni could observe staff to see if they are dealing with customers in the desired fashion

3 marks

5 • the public sector firm has a guaranteed source of income from the government whilst the private sector firm has to base its income on profits obtained
- the public sector firm often has little competition such as one hospital in an area, whilst the private sector firm has to keep advertising to ensure the customer is aware of their benefits over the competition
- the public sector firm is often the only firm in the area and so can hold a monopoly position
- the staff in the public sector firm will often accept wages which are slightly below those in the private sector, e.g. private doctors versus public sector doctors as their jobs are supposed to be more secure

4 marks

Coffee & Chords: Case Study 3

1 (a) This involves one firm (franchiser) granting another firm (franchisee) the right to trade under their name, in exchange for a fee. This fee can involve a one-off royalty payment or an annual percentage of the profits.

2 marks

(b) Benefits:
- this is a quick method of growth for *Coffee & Chords* as several franchisees can be opening at the same time without spreading Chiara and Gianni too thin in terms of time and effort
- *Coffee & Chords* will receive a percentage of the franchisee's profits
- *Coffee & Chords* have opportunities to benefit from economies of scale whereby they can run one advert but many franchisees experience an increase in sales
- the risk is shared between *Coffee & Chords* and the franchisee
- the franchisor has the power to withdraw the franchising agreement if the franchisee is not performing to the required standard

Costs:
- if one franchisee fails to perform then this could damage the reputation of the whole business, so it is difficult to maintain a corporate image
- economies of scale in advertising and bulk purchasing are not achieved in the short term and so initially this type of growth is expensive

6 marks

Exam tip: 'Discuss' means you have to write about the costs AND the benefits of this form of growth. If either the costs or the benefits are not discussed, then full marks cannot be awarded. Also the question is asking you to to relate your answers to a firm such as *Coffee & Chords* (the potential franchiser).

2 (a) This involves a firm calling in an outside firm to perform part or a whole operation, for example sending the telesales offices to India or calling in Mitie Cleaning to clean their offices, in exchange for a fee. The firm being called is sometimes referred to as a sub-contractor.

2 marks

(b) Advantages:
- the outsourcing firm is often more experienced in the operation, e.g. introducing an ICT network and so the quality of work improves
- the outsourced firm is often hired for only a short period of time and so saves the firm money in the long-term as staff are not hired on long term fixed contracts
- the firm can concentrate on its core business and leave matters such as catering or cleaning to the subcontracted business
- the firm saves money on purchasing specialised equipment that the subcontractor can provide

Disadvantages:
- the firm bears a risk that the subcontractor's work is not of the same quality as the firm's standard of work, e.g. the language problems with call centre workers in India
- the firm may have to share sensitive information with the subcontractor such as accounting which can easily be passed on to competitors
- the firm may attract some negative press from subcontracting work to a foreign company where the work was able to be carried out by British workers, e.g. call centres in India

7 marks

3 (a) A de-merger is where a firms splits into two separate listed companies. This can involve one firm selling off another part of the firm.

2 mark

(b) • as the original business is too large and is becoming inefficient and difficult to manage
  • as the firm may wish to concentrate its efforts on a smaller range of products or clients where they can specialise in this area
  • to raise money from the sale of one firm which can be reinvested in the firm

2 marks

4 • to obtain economies of scale which are the benefits from actions such as bulk buying discounts
  • to diversify, spread the risk across a greater number of products and reduce the chances of failure
  • to attract more investors who see the larger firm as less of a risk
  • a firm has the chance to dominate the market and so take advantage of control over price

4 marks

The Phatty: Case Study 1

1 • the graphics are more colourful and eye-catching
  • the figures are easier to understand as trends can be easily spotted
  • audience is able to make quick comparisons and analyse the data quickly
  • useful form of presentation when addressing a large audience or having to display figures in company literature

3 marks

2 • pictures are useful to use where an audience speaks different languages, e.g. wet floor or icons on a computer
  • useful when launching a product that is new to the market and has a new brand name, e.g. Ipod – in this case the audience saw the product in action
  • eye-catching and entertaining and is easily remembered
  • a "picture can say a thousand words" and so is more effective than explaining the benefits of the product

• effective when creating an image such as showing a personality like Duffy (singer) to attract young people to the brand

3 marks

3 • staff can raise queries about the figures and concerns are resolved instantly
  • bonds can form between members of staff which can make for a better working environment
  • instruction on new working practices are better undertaken in this fashion to ensure all staff understand what is expected of them

3 marks

4 (a) A "what if scenario" allows the firm to see the effects from introducing changes into the firm. So, if the firm were to increase price, then the spreadsheet would alter all subsequent calculations and the resulting new totals would be shown. The firm can see the forecasted changes on paper before they put them into practice.

2 marks

(b) • they perform calculations, such as averages, instantly for large columns of figures
  • graphs can be extracted from the figures to display the information in a more user friendly manner
  • "what if scenarios" can be performed which show the firm the effects of changes to the firm on paper before putting them into practice

3 marks

(c) • figures provide an accurate picture of an issue, such as '89% of the staff disagreed with the new opening hours' as opposed to 'a lot of the employees disagreed . . .'
  • comparisons can be made, especially between years e.g. profits are up 20% on last year

- calculations can be performed which offer a better insight into the firm such as 78% of the respondents were male and so that explains why football was a popular choice of article

2 marks

5 • there is formal record of written communication which can be referred back to as opposed to verbal which often relies on people's memories
   • when passing on written information everyone is given the same message as opposed to verbal communication which could be distorted in the form of "Chinese Whispers"
   • written information in the form of an internet survey would be easier to collect than a street survey where verbal communication is used in the delivery of the survey

3 marks

6 *Exam tip*: watch for repeats e.g. HP – the firm takes ownership after the last payment and leasing – where the firm doesn't take ownership. These are simply a repeat of each other and will only get 1 mark.
   • Hire purchase
     Advantage – the firm takes ownership of the printing press after its final payment, or, the firm can spead its payments over a period of time as opposed to paying for the equipment outright
     Disadvantage – the firm has to pay more money over the rental period than the price initially quoted
   • Leasing
     Advantage – the firm can change the press easily if it is broken or obsolete
     Disadvantage – the firm does not retain this equipment as an asset
   • Bank Loan
     Advantage – the firm can get relatively quick access to the funds
     Disadvantage – a small firm like *The Phatty* would have to pay potentially higher interest rates on their loan

4 marks

7 *Exam tip*: Note this is an "explain" question and so the effects on the firm have to be mentioned.
   • competition – a leading magazine such as *NME* could launch their own upgraded magazine which would reduce *The Phatty*'s sales
   • socio-cultural – people could alter their reading habits and prefer to catch this kind of news online and so newspapers lose their appeal
   • recession – people may lack the disposable income to purchase items like this so and *The Phatty* may have problems finding advertisers

2 marks

The Phatty: Case Study 2

1 • through a survey the firm can get an up to date profile of their customers interests and criticisms which keeps the firm in touch with the latest trends
   • any surveys or questionnaires will likely provide information that is highly relevant to the firm's needs and so will be very useful
   • the data collected on the readers tastes and preferences is unique to *The Phatty* and so does not have to be shared with the competition and could give them a competitive edge
   • the accuracy of the information is easy to check as the firm is responsible for collecting it and so can check errors in surveys which makes it very reliable

4 marks

2 *Note: This is also an "explain" question so the effects on the firm have to be discussed. The "value" means the question needs to consider the good and bad points.*

Benefits:
   • a wide range of information sources can be accessed which means *The Phatty* has a good cross section of information to support their decisions
   • it is often cheap to collect which will leave the firm money to invest in more detailed primary research

Costs:

- the information is often not directly related to the firm's purpose and so has limited relevance to the firm's needs
- often this research is out of date and so the firm has to be cautious as they may be basing decisions on trends that have changed
- the accuracy of the information is difficult to check, for example, sample size, and so there is a risk the information is misleading or at worst inaccurate
- a firm's competitors can also get access to secondary information which means they may be first to spot and exploit gaps in the market
- the information can be biased as it has been collected by another source which may make it misleading to the firm

6 marks

3 Decision-making
- *The Phatty* decided on certain links with ticket agencies websites as based on their surveys of customers

Identifying new business opportunities
- a survey of customers using the firm's database helps to identify what the customer wants

Measuring the performance of the business
- the response to promotional campaigns was used to gauge the popularity of certain restaurants

Monitoring the performance of the firm
- the managers of *The Phatty* monitored the performance of journalists through readers responses to articles

4 marks

4 Internal info

Costs:
- this information is incomplete as it does not give an indication of how the competition is performing
- costs of setting up the systems to collect the information can be high

Benefits:
- easy and quick to access
- the accuracy of the information can be checked e.g. a mistake in a question in a survey which could have altered the results

External info

Costs:
- may be out of date
- information can be biased or unreliable
- competitors can get access

Benefits:
- a firm gets the chance to appreciate the PESTec factors that influence a firm such as the interest rates going up and potentially increasing costs
- a wide range of information is accessed which helps to support decision-making

6 marks

5 Data Protection Act 1998
- firms holding information on customers, suppliers and staff must register with the Infomation Commissioner and state the purpose of holding the information
- firms must reveal the information if requested by an individual who has a right to access the information held about them and can claim compensation if it is proved to be inaccurate
- firms may only hold information for a lawful purpose
- firms must keep the information up to date and accurate, for example, when points are removed from a driver's licence, then the firm has to alter its records
- firms have to take measures to ensure the information is stored safely to prevent unauthorised, inapproporiate access
- firms may not hold information for longer than is necessary

5 marks

Note the Computer Misuse Act 1990 relates to the use of computers and so is not directly relevant to the idea of handling information.

The Phatty: Case Study 3

1 Powerpoint:
- the editor was able to communicate the change in direction (objectives) of the paper via a powerpoint presentation, which can be delivered to a large audience at once or stored and revisited later by colleagues

Emails:
- staff could instantly send large amounts of communcation to a wide range of recipients
- staff were able to work from the comfort of their own home, during hours of their own choice, as all of the firm's correspondence could be accessed and stored via email

Video Conferencing:
- this allowed more regular meetings beween The Phatty's staff and the ICT firm, thereby allowing more face to face meetings where images or designs could be discussed at length

Databases:
- customers details can be stored and sorted to produce lists, for example, on average age of the subscribers – giving the firm a more informed profile of their customers
- advertising should be more effective as it can then be tailored to meet the behaviour of the customer such as mail shots to their email addresses showing the latest promotions

Website:
- the firm was able to offer links to music festival sites, which would allow customers to view prices with the option to buy
- online surveys gave the firm up to date information on their customers

7 marks

2 Costs:
- morale may fall as staff feel their jobs are at risk

- technical support needs to be organised which may require restructuring of the firm, e.g. a new department
- costs of purchasing, installing and maintaining the equipment
- new skillls are required such as handling and analysing the information which requires retraining of staff and time off work
- many new systems present teething problems which, unless handled well, can damage the reputation of the firm

Benefits:
- large amounts of information are produced more quickly, e.g. through online surveys which allow a firm like *The Phatty* to be more up to date with trends
- floor space is saved, e.g. *The Phatty* changed to smaller premises, as files are saved on computers and not cabinets and producion lines were replaced with computers
- money was saved, for example, with the use of video conferencing equipment thereby avoided any travelling costs
- the firm's overall efficiency (i.e. less wastage) is improved, e.g. emails allowed instant communication and the editors could easily monitor the various websites

8 marks

3
- the staff may be reluctant to adopt the technology as it could result in redundancies in the firm
- the firm may lack the funds to purchase, install and maintain the technology
- managers may lack the knowledge to select an appropriate system and the skills to ensure it is fully implemented and up to date with changes
- the software can be at risk of viruses which can halt a production line which is highly interdependent, e.g. the machines are all connected and a disruption to one area can have an effect on another area – a virus on the webpage would halt *The Phatty*'s business completely

4 marks

4 Staff:
  • staff can acquire a wider range of skills which allows them to multi-task, e.g. a machine operator can order the raw materials and oversee production lines
  • staff, however, can also become de-skilled, whereby machines replace labour, for example when carrying out quality checks, and so staff can become demoralised
  • staff relations may deteriorate as they increasingly communicate via emails and lose personal contact – this can prevent staff from forming a team and offering support for each other
  • staff may opt to work at home (teleworking) and simply use the offices as a place for meetings
  • staff will have to undergo training which is demanding for some workers, e.g. women returning to work after maternity leave

Firm:
  • the structure of the firm can change from a hierarchical to a flat structure as managers as able to monitor a greater number of people in a shorter period of time, e.g. Head of Maths monitoring 5 Maths teacher's gradebooks on the database
  • this greater ease of monitoring can allow more work to be delegated away from the Head Office and so a firm can decentralise a lot of their work
  • staff may be made redundant, which cuts a firm's labour costs, but can result in demotivated workforce
  • departments or positions may have to be created such as an ICT technician

6 marks

Head2Head: Case Study 1

1 • recession was looming
  • reluctance of males to visit the salons
  • larger firms can quickly copy their idea
  • larger firms have more financial clout and management expertise

4 marks

2 • strategic decision – is a long term decision which sets out a vision for the business and is made by the owners of the firm, for example, *Head2Head*'s aim was one of growth
  • tactical decision – this is a medium term decision which puts the strategic decision into practise and is made by the middle managers, for example, Craig has decided to target the male clients as a way of achieving growth
  • operational decision – are short term decisions and generally respond to the day to day matters of the firm. Most junior managers make these decisions, for example changing the rota for staff

6 marks

3 Strengths:
  • *Head2Head* offer low prices which would beat the competition
  • distinctive brand name

Weaknesses:
  • lack of skilled staff
  • shortage of staff

Opportunities:
  • gap in the market for male grooming
  • survey of London had been positive which could make its way up to Scotland

Threats:
  • competitors have more cash to copy this idea on a bigger scale
  • competitiors have the management experise that *Head2Head* lacks
  • recession looming

8 marks

4 It was a good idea but as they lacked the cash and experience to put it into practice they perhaps should have gained more advice and information on this area. They should have taken more time planning their decision and anticipating problems.
You have the choice to say yes or no here so long as it is fully justified.

2 marks

5 • the firm may lack the necessary finance to make the investments necessary for the decision to be a success
  • staff may lack the experience or managerial skills to put a decision into practice
  • staff may be reluctant to take a decision on as it could result in them losing a job
  • the firm may lack the proper technology such as an intranet to adopt the decision effectively

5 marks

Head2Head: Case Study 2

1 Identify the problem:
  • Donna and Craig had to grow or risk being overtaken by their competitors in the market

Identify the objectives:
  • Donna and Craig could have set aims such as to increase profits and improve the standard of service which would give the business a focus over the next year

Gather the information:
  • Donna and Craig would have to gather information on how they would achieve these aims, such as addressing more closely the feedback from customers and competitors efforts in this market

Analyse the information:
  • Donna and Craig would have to set aside quality time to analyse this information in terms of possible costs to training staff and purchasing new equipment

Devise possible solutions:
  • Before committing fully to their decision Donna and Craig would have to consider if any alternatives existed such as abandoning the idea altogether or introducing male products gradually into their existing salons

Select the best solution:
  • Donna and Craig would have to select from all their options which alternative to pursue

Communicate the decision:
  • Having made their decision, Donna and Craig would commuciate it to the rest of their staff such as via a company newsletter

Implement the decision:
  • Donna and Craig would proceed with their decison such as training staff to improve service or negotiating better discounts with suppliers to reduce costs and increase profits

Evaluate the effectiveness of the decision:
  • Donna and Craig could check acounts to see if profits rose or customer feedback to see if the quality of the service improved

9 marks

2 • the firm takes time to gather the right information and analyse it fully and so no knee jerk reactions are made such as closing a shop when it is simply experiencing poor seasonal sales
  • each decision is made using relevant information which means decisions should be more effective such as expanding a service that is popular with the clients
  • alternative solutions are considered which means the firm does not simply jump at the first solution they thought of, for example, extending the Friday opening hours at the start of the month when most people have been paid as opposed to every Friday
  • a structured decision-making model allows the staff to get involved at relevant points and logically follow the decision through to its completion. This will bring an order to the decision

4 marks

3 • not all decisions require this level of analysis which means gut reactions to problems could be overlooked
  • the use of these models may slow the decision process down which means the firm may lose out to to the competition who have been quicker to get their ideas onto the market

- being presented with many alternatives to a problem is often difficult to carry out in practice which can leave Donna and Craig swamped with too many solutions
- analysis of data such as handling the EPOS information or sorting the database files may require training which costs time and money and eats into revenue and profits

4 marks

4
- train staff to give them a better understanding of their jobs which should improve the quality of their decisions
- encourage staff to adopt decision-making techniques that will bring a structure and logical process to their decision-making
- ensuring staff have access to up to date information such as the customers' reviews which must be circulated promptly round the firm
- managers should be encouraged to take risks whereby failure will not result in dismissal but instead a thorough evaluation and identification of the factors that held back success
- create a culture where staff are consulted and encouraged to give their input which should result in them being more willing to accept the decisions made by their managers
- seek advice from experts such as Business Gateway on handling major decisions such as restructuring

5 marks

5
- economic – the recession could force customers to cut back on luxury purchases such as visits to a salon
- socio-cultural – the press were critical of male grooming which could influence the decision of many males to pay attention to improving their appearance and so hold it back from becoming a popular mainstream trend
- competitors may have adopted the trend far more quickly and effectively than *Head2Head*

3 marks

Head2Head: Case Study 3

1
- Planning
  A manager would set out the aims of the firm, for example, when Craig planned to increase their sales by 5% over the next 2 years
- Organising
  A manager would have to ensure all resources were in the correct place to enable decisions to be carried out effectively such as ensuring each salon was properly stocked with shampoo, lotions and towels
- Commanding
  A manager has to give out instruction to their staff in the same manner that Donna had to outline the staff rota
- Controlling
  A manager would monitor the performance of a firm just as Craig monitored the sales performance of each shop to keep him informed should anything go wrong such as a drop in sales due to poor service
- Coordinating
  A manager has to ensure all departments are working towards the same goal. Donna, for example, gave each of the salons a goal of obtaining 10 new clients a week
- Delegating
  A manager would pass on their authority to carry out certain tasks. The beauticians were delegated the role of training
- Motivating
  A manager would try to get the best from their staff through initiatives such as rewarding successful salons with a bottle of champagne

8 marks

2
- check the till receipts to see if sales have increased
- check the database to see if clients numbers were increasing, which would suggest an increase in customer loyalty

- check website reviews to see if the number of clients complaints have decreased which suggests service is improving
- reading reviews in newspapers/magazines would also confirm if the salon was achieving a more favourable public image
- check the number of staff achieving their training accreditation to assure Donna that the quality of their service was improving
- compare monthly profits to confirm if the salons were keeping a better control of their costs

5 marks

3 • strategic decision – is a long term decision which sets out a vision for the business and is made by the owners or the senior managers of the firm, for example, *Head2Head*'s aim was to increase sales by 5% over the next 2 years
- tactical decision – this is a medium term decision which puts the strategic decision into practice and is made by the middle managers, for example, Craig has decided to monitor more closely the performance of each salon
- operational decision – a short term decision which generally responds to the day to day matters of the firm. Most junior managers make these decisions, for example, checking each day the stocks of shampoo and towels or arranging for cover for a member of staff

6 marks

4 • networked tills would allow Donna and Craig to monitor the sales performance of each salon and so any decisions could be related in direct response to problems in this area
- database of clients allowed Donna and Craig to select the right type of promotion to suit their clients, e.g. discounts for students and more up-market products for professional sportsmen

- databases would allow Donna and Craig to decide which staff had received their accreditation to ensure the standards of quality were maintained
- EPOS systems allows Donna and Craig to keep control of the stock and only make re-ordering decisions when necessary
- EPOS systems would allow Donna and Craig to spot trends in the sales of certain products which would make their purchasing decisions more effective
- e-newsletters emailed to all staff would ensure any decisions such as new grooming products were communicated to all staff and staff were, in general, kept up to date with all decisions
- websites would allow Donna and Craig to view customer comments which would allow them to review very quickly the impact of their decisions

6 marks

SmoothEEz: Case Study 1

1 • the firm may aim to simply survive, i.e. to break even as the firm has not yet established a loyal customer base
- sales maximisation – the firm may have aimed to increase sales by reaching a greater number of their clients via a greater number of outlets
- social responsibilty – the firm may aim to provide healthy drinks as an alternative to sugary, carbonated drinks
- growth – the firm may aim to expand its product range by introducing new flavours

4 marks

2 Advantages:
- as staff are grouped into departments, such as a design department, they have the opportunity to specialise in their area, which should raise the overall quality of their output
- this is a very clear structure and so staff are certain of their role within the firm, i.e. they work in engineering or legal department

- it allows each department to be accountable for their results, e.g. the quality of production
- it is suitable for the organisation of large firms
- less chance of duplicating resources

Disadvantages:
- departments can often put their interests before those of the whole firm
- it is difficult to coordinate as many activities involve several departments and communication between departments is not as good as communication within departments, i.e. it can become bureaucratic
- as comunication between departments can be difficult it means the firm is not responsive to change

6 marks

3 (a)
- 70% of the firm's business was taken up by 3 main clients
- each customer had specific needs that required special attention
- the firm was expanding and was in the process of changing its location

2 marks

(b) Advantages:
- personal attention allowed the customers'needs to be met in a more effective manner, e.g. a unique invoicing and purchasing system for the supermarket
- customer loyalty builds up which guarantees future business
- the firm is often able to charge a higher price due to the personal attention
- the firm has the opportunity to learn valuable commercial skills from the larger clients such analysing the research data form the supermarket's loyalty card

Disadvantages:
- there is a chance there will be the duplication of admin, sales and accounting to support each customer which will increase costs

- there are fewer chances for economies of scale with bulk purchasing, for instance of packaging, as each customer has their own unique design
- as each customer has their own unique demands it may be difficult to coordinate across many customers, e.g. the supermarket priorites are packaging whilst the warehouse is more concerned about *SmoothEEz's* investment in advertising
- absences cannot be covered by staff who are working on different clients as they are not accustomed to their needs

6 marks

4 (a) This involves the firm grouping its staff by the product or service they produce, e.g. a firm producing transport vehicles could offer rental of cars for private use or rental of buses for commercial use.

1 mark

(b) Advantages:
- staff can acquire specialist knowledge on their product which enhances motivation which should improve the quality of decision-making
- with more in-depth understanding of their clients, the firm can become more responsive to changes in the marketplace
- it is easy for the firm to identify areas (or products) that are underperforming with appropriate action undertaken
- objectives such as profit maximisation can be easy to achieve across the different product groupings

Disadvantages:
- there may be duplication of activities across each of the product groupings such as marketing or accounting
- divisions may begin to compete with each other which can be counterproductive, i.e. not sharing good practice

6 marks

SmoothEEz: Case Study 2

1 An entrepreneurial structure is one where decisions are made by a few managers at the core of the firm, such as an advertising agency.

maximum 2 marks

Advantages:
- decision are made quickly as staff do not have to be consulted
- staff know who to go to with any problems and to whom they are accountable

maximum 2 marks

2 Advantages:
- staff were able to specialise in their departments and roles are very clear
- managers are appointed to oversee each department and so each member of staff can be monitored and managed fully
- a lot of delegation takes place which relieves the workload of the founders and allows them to focus on the strategic decisions within the firm

Disadvantages:
- the chain of command is longer and so decisions take time to be approved and implemented
- the longer chain of command may result in the "Chinese Whispers" effect whereby messages are distorted and implemented incorrectly
- communication may be slowed as it has to pass though many layers of authority and so the firm may lose touch with its customers' needs
- changes are difficult to implement and so the firm fails to stay up with market trends

4 marks

3 Advantages:
- workers are given more responsibility and so feel more empowered
- a shorter chain of command allows information to pass up the firm more quickly which allows more informed and also more effective decision-making
- the firm can become more responsive to market changes and so keeps up with market trends

- the firm may save money on wages by removing a layer of management
- this structure is appropriate for small to medium sized firms and allows them to achieve their best results

4 marks

4
- size – if the firm is small it is unlikely to have a hierarchical structure with many layers of authority and departments, whereas a public sector firm such as a hospital which is highly accountable to the public would favour a hierarchical structure
- the product – if the firm has a wide range of products it is likely to favour a team approach like a matrix structure where each product can be managed independently with control over its own budgets
- staff – if the firm has many highly skilled staff, e.g. in a university faculty, then the firm is likely to favour a flat structure where there is high degree of delegation and trust on the members of staff
- customer – if the customer has many unique needs then the firm may decentralise a lot of the decision-making

3 marks

5 Advantages:
- changes are easier to introduce across the whole firm as all decisions are flowing out from the head office and there is less need for consultation
- it is easy to promote a corporate image as procedures and paperwork can all be standardised so every site is following the same instructions
- the firm can engage in bulk buying of raw materials such as fruit as they can gather the figures in one place
- head office is likely to be a large function where the more experienced managers are hired, thereby improving the effectiveness of their decisions
- it promotes strong leadership and so is a very beneficial structure to have in times of crisis

Disadvantages:
- workers may feel removed from head office as they are not consulted on matters
- prospective managers in the firm may lack the necessary experience for promotion
- head office may lack the required knowledge for local conditions which can make their decision making ineffective
- there is a very large responsibility on workers at head office which can cause high stress levels

6 marks

6 • plan – managers will set out the aims of the restructuring such as improving the service to customers
- organise – Adam will have to ensure the resources are all in the right place for this restructuring, e.g. each division has the right ICT to cope with their new customers
- command – Adam will instruct the staff on their new responsibilities such as being in charge of purchasing for the supermarket
- coordinate – Adam will make sure everyone in the firm is following the same goal of improving the service to customers by meeting up with all the divisions and ensuring they are clear on ways of achieving this
- control – Adam will monitor if the restructuring is a success by asking the customers for their opinions on the quality of service
- delegate – Adam will give staff authority to carry out tasks such as recruiting new staff
- motivate – Adam will aim to get the best out of all his staff through initiatives such as team working, social events or bonuses

4 marks

SmoothEEz: Case Study 3

1 These are the values, beliefs and norms relating to the company or organisation that are shared by all its staff.

2 marks

(b) • signage on all the mugs, posters
- passing an e-newsletter round the firm
- introducing staff uniforms
- having a corporate colour scheme
- inter-company competitions to acknowledge the café with the highest sales

5 marks

(c) • staff relationships improve which means staff are able to work as a team and share ideas
- employees feel part of the firm which should lead to a low staff turnover
- staff should feel more motivated about their work and so absenteeism should fall
- staff should become loyal to the firm and offer a greater commitment to projects
- staff are happier, more assured of their place in the firm, therefore are likely to be more productive

5 marks

2 (a) This involves a manager passing on responsibility to their subordinates to carry out certain tasks. Also seen as delegation.

2 marks

(b) staff were entrusted to:
- decide their weekly food orders in response to customer demands
- monitor their staff on matters such as time keeping
- design in store publicity such as adverts on the shop windows

3 marks

(c) • staff who are closer to the customers and so should make decisions that are directly beneficial to them and so are more effective
- as staff have more control over their jobs they should be more motivated and so less likely to be absent
- staff can acquire a greater range of skills which should make them more experienced for management

- senior management are relieved of certain tasks and so can focus on the strategic decisions within the firm
- it creates more possibilities for creative ideas which should result in better communication between staff

5 marks

(d) • employees are often given more work to do for the same amount of money which could be received negatively
- managers may be reluctant to give up some decision-making as it could question their workloads or purpose
- staff have to be trained to make certain decisions which is costly
- empowerment often occurs when a firm has flattened their structure following redundancies and so staff may be see it as the firm getting the same output for less money which results in a degree of cynicism of this extra responsibility

3 marks

T in the Bag: Case Study 1

1 (a) This is a process where firms first establish the customers' needs through market research and then allows these needs to influence the direction of the business.

2 marks

(b) • firm can identify customers' needs and so spot trends/changes in the market quickly
- firms are more likely to sell a product or service that customers want
- satisfying customer needs increases a firm's chances of making a sale and achieving profits
- better chance of securing customer loyalty

3 marks

2 (a) *(1 mark each)*
- telephone/postal/street surveys
- group discussions
- hall test
- customer audits
- observation (e.g. CCTV)
- test marketing
- use of technology – EPOS/loyalty cards/digital TV

4 marks

(b)

Method	Advantages	Disadvantages
Telephone/postal/ street surveys	• Wide area is covered • Cheap to undertake • Responses are immediate (telephone) • Responses can be clarified (telephone and street) • Certain respondents can be targeted	• Response rates are low • Customers see it as an intrusion (telephone) • No guarantee the respondent has filled it in (postal) • Interviewers have to be trained which costs money • Subject to interviewer bias (street)

Continued ➔

Method	Advantages	Disadvantages
Group discussions	• Opinions and attitudes can be collected • Consumers behaviour can be observed and analysed • 2-way communication can be undertaken so points are clarified	• Consumers are sometimes influenced by their peers and so their comments are made in line with the dominant group member • Difficult to analyse the opinions collected
Hall test	• Instant reactions to products can be gathered • Consumers can be targeted e.g. young mums in a supermarket • Relatively cheap to undertake	• Only a small sample is accessed which may not reflect the views of the market • Can be difficult to analyse qualitative information
Customer audits	• Information is very up to date and trends are easy to spot	• Consumers are not always good at keeping diaries up to date and so results can be inaccurate
Observation (e.g. CCTV)	• A large number of consumers can be observed in a short space of time • Consumers are behaving naturally and so results are reliable	• Can be difficult to explain the behaviour witnessed e.g. why have people avoided that display? • The external factors influencing behaviour have to be considered, e.g. weather
Test marketing	• Problems can be identified before a national launch which saves the firm a lot of money • Changes to the product can be made in response to customers reactions in real scenarios, e.g. the eco brand may simply be too expensive	• Competitors may get wind of your new product • Regional preferences may not be reflective of other parts of the country e.g. English opinion of Irn Bru may not be as favourable as Scottish
Use of technology EPOS/Loyalty cards/ Digital TV	• Results are instant • Collection by electronic means makes analysis easier as links with charts and graphs packages are possible • The firm has a lot of background information and can cross-reference purchases with occupation and postcodes giving insightful profiles	• Expensive to set up electronic systems to record data • Often useful to large chains of shops • Requires manager who are skilled at analysing numbers which can be expensive

8 marks

3 (a) Desk research is the collection of data that had already been collated for another purpose and is often published. Examples include Annual Reports, Mintel Reports and government publications such as Social Trends. It can be internal to the firm (sales reports) or external to the firm (unemployment figures).

2 marks

(b) • There are a wide range of sources to access so decisions should be more informed
• the information is often cheap to collect so costs will be low
• competitors information is available to access so the firm has a fuller understanding of the whole market
• saves the firm a lot of time carrying out the research if the information has already been collected which frees up time for analysis of the data

2 marks

4 Advantages:
• the firm can often charge a high price as the product is exclusive
• the firm doesn't face a lot of competition from the large multinationals as there are fewer opportunities to make the scale of sales they would normally achieve with the mass markets
• the firm can build up an expertise in this area which enhances their image of quality

Disadvantages:
• there is high risk of failure as the firm often has a limited product portfolio and so in times of crisis has only a few products to rely on
• the products can be easily copied by the multinationals and often for a lower price which dilutes the exclusive image of the product

4 marks

T in the Bag: Case Study 2

1 • product range was too wide which left unsold stock – note latter point is operations so can't be used on its own
• prices too high could lose out on future sales
• poor market research – so not enough data has been collected
• segmenting the market was difficult and failed to maximise sales

4 marks

2 (a) • charge a high price
• product line extensions are easier
• build up a loyal customer base
• brand can be easily copied
• expensive to establish in terms of advertising

4 marks

(b) • new product line extension e.g. hoodies
• new outlet for sales e.g. sports shops
• new advertising medium, move from word of mouth to magazines
• new pricing strategy e.g. introduce a competitive method to avoid a price war

4 marks

(c) • spreads the risk if one product fails there are others to rely
• easier to manage, i.e. different strategies for different stages
• firm attracts different segments of the market so maximises sales
• the large size of the firm attracts more investors

3 marks

3 (a) • price penetration – low then high
• promotional pricing – low for a short period of time
• competitive – same as competition to avoid a price war
• destroyer – but point out their design is unique and they are small so reserves are low
• not premium or skimming

4 marks

(b) Benefits:
- maximise profits from high price
- catch the early adopters – technical way of saying those who want to be seen as first with the product

Costs:
- could lose out on sales as product price is too high
- loss of status as product is lowered in price

2 marks

4 *Note this is an "explain" question so an effect or consequence is needed for the full marks.*
- the right price is selected for each segment which can allow the firm to achieve its correct objectives such an maximum profit
- the correct design is chosen for the product which can distinguish the product from the competition
- the correct place is selected for the product which allows the firm to reach its target audience
- the firm has an effective advertising campaign as it does not advertise in the wrong place for the customer

4 marks

T in the Bag: Case Study 3

1 TV:
- expensive
- reaches a national audience

Internet:
- can be placed in the view of the target audience, easily updated
- ad may be ignored

Magazines:
- colour images have impact, can be kept for future reference
- may be over-looked

Outdoor media:
- can attract several target audiences
- can suffer weather deterioration, subject to vandalism

Newspapers (depends on the circulation):
- cheap, reach national audience, good for local audiences
- often not scrutinised, no sound and movement

Direct mail:
- can be tailored to suit the audience
- can be seen as junk mail

8 marks

2 (a) Where a manufacturer encourages a wholesaler or retailer to stock their product.

1 mark

(b) • point of sale materials
- sale or return
- dealer competitions
- credit facilities
- staff training
- dealer loaders

4 marks

3 Internet selling:
- reach global audience, open 24 hours, compile a database with info collected
- customers reluctant to give out private information, not practical with some products e.g. local purchases of bread/milk
- Mail order:
  - cheap and saves on shop overheads, customers can make use of the credit facilities not always available in high street shops
  - lack of personal contact, customers can run up bad debt, can incur large delivery charges

4 marks

4 (a) • product itself – a designer t-shirt wants to be sold in exclusive outlets
- finance available to the firm – a lot of funds means the firm can advertise heavily which encourages the wholesalers and retailers to stock their products

- reliability of the intermediary – an unreliable or poor quality wholesaler may encourage the manufacturer to sell direct to the customer over the internet
- government restrictions e.g. selling medicines in a pharmacy
- stage on the product life cycle – e.g. the product is likely to be popular in the maturity stage and so will be sold in many outlets
- manufacturers' distribution capabilities – e.g. an owner of a fleet of vans will likely deliver the goods themselves
- intended market – e.g. selling abroad may require the use of an agent

2 marks

(b)
- acts as an intermediary for the manufacturer and retailer
- offers training to the retailer
- can repackage the goods for the manufacturer
- ensures the manufacturer reaches a wider range of customers

4 marks

5 *Note this question needs a description of the effects of the sponsorship.*
- raises awareness of the product which can increase brand loyalty
- product can be seen on the re-runs of the sporting events which is free publicity for the firm
- the firm can be associated with the event it is sponsoring, e.g. t-shirts and a healthy lifestyle, which boosts sales

2 marks

Pizz-A-Fun: Case Study 1

1
- the firm's list of suppliers was too large
- supplier of cheese was unreliable
- surplus stock level was increasing storage costs
- staff stealing the surplus stock

4 marks

2 A supplier could be judged on:
- the prices or possible discounts for bulk purchases which impacts on costs
- credit terms on offer which helps *Pizz-A-Fun* spread their repayments
- quality of goods which will influence how the product is viewed
- reliability to ensure late deliveries are not an issue
- ICT compatability to gauge if, for example, edi links can be established
- location to ensure the goods are not subject to time delays
- after sales service to ensure *Pizz-A-Fun* has someone on hand quickly should a problem arise

5 marks

3 (a)
- high storage costs such as air conditioning or refrigeration costs for the food
- some stock may deteriorate such as food
- some stock may fall out of fashion, such as turkey meat after Christmas
- money is tied up in the stock, i.e. *Pizz-A-Fun* have paid their suppliers but haven't got the money from sales, and this money could have been used for advertising or training staff
- space is been taken up that could have been used as another production line
- staff may be tempted to help themselves to the surplus stock

4 marks

(b)
- the firm may simply have to turn away customers and so lose existing and future sales
- the firm is unable to cope with an unexpected order e.g. from a supermarket
- the firm may have to stop production which costs the firm money as managerial staff wages are still being paid with no output and it also takes time to restart the machines to have them recalibrated etc.

- to resolve stock shortages a firm may have to buy in stock at short notice from a supplier where they are likely to be charged the full retail price
- as the firm is in general buying smaller quantities, they are missing out on bulk buying discounts

4 marks

4 (a) This describes a process where firms seek to reduce stock of raw materials and instead have them delivered to the firm "just in time" for the stock to be used on the production line. Firms also aim to have zero stock of finished goods and will aim only to produce in response to customers' orders.

2 marks

(b) *Note this is an explain question so the effects on Pizz-A-Fun have to be explained.*

Exam tip: these answers are very similar to those detailed for having too low stock.

Benefits:
- space is freed up as the firm's stock levels are reduced so the firm can open up a new production line
- as money is not tied up in stock then cash flow improves and releases funds for advertising
- the firm has to develop close bonds with its supplier and so relations here are very much improved
- the previous point demands that the firm reduce the number of suppliers which become easier to manage
- the responsibility for holding the stock and dealing with breakages and deterioration is placed with the supplier which means they are liable to cover these costs

Costs:
- responsibility of checking quality is with the supplier and so the firm has to place a lot of trust that they will carry this out fully and will have to face the

consequences if they don't
- stock is delivered more frequently in smaller batches which increases the admin costs and number of deliveries to the factory
- if the supplier is late then the whole production line may halt which is costly to start again
- the JIT set up is not responsive to short term changes in demand and so the firm may be out of step with market trends
- with many small orders being placed with the supplier the firm my lose out on any bulk buying discounts

6 marks

Pizz-A-Fun: Case Study 2

1
- groups of products can be changed to alter the flavours, in this case, of pizzas
- some bulk purchases can be made which allows for bulk buying discounts
- the products can appeal to a greater number of market segments
- workers are able to specialise in an area of the production, such as packaging of the pizzas, which cuts the cost of expensive staff
- machinery can be relatively standardised which reduces the overall cost of the machinery

4 marks

2
- labour costs are high due to the staff being highly specialised
- bulk buying purchases are not always possible
- as the goods are made to the customers' requirements the firm needs to obtain a variety of machinery which is expensive
- the firm will often take a long period of time to produce the good which may work against the supplier

4 marks

3 Advantages:
- firms achieve economies of scale through producing large quantities of the product

which lowers their unit costs

- large quantities of the product can be produced which means volume sales and high profits
- often the production line is highly automated which involves the use of many machines which avoid any labour costs/disputes and can be run for 24 hours

Disadvantages:

- the product can be highly standardised which reduces the level of variety for the customer
- workers may lack a high degree of motivation as the job is very repetitive
- the production line involves large investment by the firm
- if the production line breaks down it is very costly as each part is very dependent on the next stage of the line

6 marks

4 • job production – wedding cake, bridges or web pages
- batch production – chocolate, bread, housing estates
- flow production – cars

3 marks

5 • product – most foodstuffs are transported in this fashion to allow for refrigeration
- legal restrictions – lorry drivers have had their driving hours restricted and so it may be quicker to transport via the train
- cost – it is relatively expensive to transport goods via the air and so may be reserved for one-off expensive products
- location – if the customer is based abroad then the firm may decide to use sea freight where ports are easily accessed
- customer demands – if the firm has to deliver to a supermarket's warehouse then using road freight may give the firm easier access to the supplier

5 marks

6 • database – this would help the firm to monitor its stock
- satellite monitoring – where lorries can be traced at any point and customers can track their stock
- Edi links where orders can be raised automatically with *Pizz-A-Fun* when stocks of pizzas in the supermarkets fall below a certain level
- costing the supermarket's order for pizzas can be done on a spreadsheet

2 marks

7 • raises awareness of *Pizz-A-Fun*'s brand name
- a source of free advertising

1 mark

Pizz-A-Fun: Case Study 3

1 • quality assurance – where the pizzas are checked at various stages on the production line to ensure they comply with the firms standards
- quality control – where the finished pizzas are checked for mistakes before they are sent to the customer
- quality circles – where volunteers from the workforce meet up regularly, with a manager present, to discuss issues directly associated with their work
- benchmarking – where the firm sets its own standards against the industry leader
- total quality management – involves every area of the firm being investigated to identify where quality can be improved

4 marks

2 Costs:
- workers are not producing any output whilst they are attending the quality circles
- manager have to be trained to handle the groups which can cost money and time
- if the group is not managed well then worker's complaints will dominate and the issue of solutions can be overlooked

Answers

- management has to be seen to be responding to the workers concerns by implementing their suggestions or changing practices at some level otherwise the workers will see the exercise as pointless

Benefits:
- workers get a chance to voice their concerns which can help to alleviate their worries
- if the workers suggestions are being seen to be put into practice then this will raise morale greatly
- management stay in touch with the operational problems of the business which they are often removed from
- managers and workers get a chance to communicate about issues directly linked with their work which should improve employee relations
- there is a quick identification of the firm's problems and consequently a quick solution

6 marks

3
- team working – teams will allow problems to be shared and for a greater pool of solutions to be raised as opposed to one member of staff settling an issue on their own
- seeking customers views – the firm actively seeks the opinions of its stakeholders and is receptive to criticisms
- zero defects – the firm introduces a policy of "getting it right first time and every time" amongst all workers

2 marks

4 A firm:
- opportunity to charge a higher price which will increase profits
- better chance of loyal customers because the product is more trusted
- reduces the number of customer complaints because errors in the product have been removed

- reduces the number of mistakes and avoids costs associated with waste because of better process and quality control
- conforms to the industry standards for the production of chocolate which means a bigger market is reached

A customer:
- builds up confidence in the brand because quality is better
- customers achieve a higher level of satisfaction from the product as there are no mistakes

4 marks

5 (a)
- hourly rate – this is a time rate method of payment and involves workers being paid on the hours they have worked. Workers have no incentive to improve quality at this stage as output is not a factor of their wages
- piece rate – workers are paid on the amount of goods they have produced. This is linked to quality as managers could refuse to pay workers for goods declared faulty

2 marks

(b)
- flat rate – this involves managers being paid a salary, which is paid monthly and expressed as a yearly sum. Management and professional workers such as lawyers or teachers are often paid in this fashion
- overtime – workers are paid for the extra hours they work which are over and above their contracted hours. This is often paid in line with the number of "extra" hours worked with a rate that is better then the normal rate, e.g. "double time"
- commission – many workers will be paid a small basic rate of pay with the opportunity to add to this via the commission the workers make from a sale. This commission is worked out as a percentage of the value of the sale made by the employee

3 marks

6 (a) this is a strategic objective for the firm as it sets out a general vision for the factory and it was made by senior management

2 marks

(b) • to change their suppliers to obtain better quality raw materials
     • to introduce methods such as quality circles that will help achieve an overall improvement in quality
     • to introduce training for all staff in order to raise an awareness of quality

2 marks

2Fit Gym: Case Study 1

1 • gym membership has fallen
   • poor record-keeping meant chasing unpaid bills was difficult
   • Bob has been refused a bank loan
   • overall poor management of Bob's costs

3 marks

2 (a) • borrowing at a high interest rate
       • not chasing unpaid bills
       • taking too many drawings
       • low sales
       • purchasing equipment rather than leasing it

5 marks

(b) • arrange a bank overdraft/bank loan
     • chase unpaid bills
     • try to extend your credit with supplier
     • seek out a cheaper supplier
     • reduce drawings
     • encourage customers to pay by direct debit
     • instead of purchasing equipment, arrange a lease

5 marks

3 Working capital:
   • this is calculated by subtracting the current liabilities from the current assets and it shows how liquid a firm is, i.e. how easy it is for a firm to pay its short term debts

Creditors:
   • these are the persons to whom the firm owes money, e.g. suppliers

Current assets
   • these are items the firms own and are likely to change value within the year

Current liabilities
   • these represent the bills the firm owes, normally to its suppliers

4 marks

4 • fall in sales
   • rise in the suppliers raw material costs

2 marks

5 • lease equipment rather than purchase it
   • reduce wages by banning overtime
   • employ more energy efficient initiatives such as light sensitive lighting in the gyms to reduce electrcity bill
   • borrow when there is a more favourbale interest rate

3 marks

6 • increase its cash/bank
   • increase the number of debtors
   • increase the sales (and increase the number of debtors)
   • reduce the number of liabilities i.e. pay off your creditors
   • sell off a fixed asset e.g. machines

3 marks

2Fit Gym: Case Study 2

1 Ratios allow a firm to:
   • compare their performance with their competitors or other firms
   • compare their performance with last years results
   • identify a trend in their profits such as a continuous rise in expenses
   • identify problems with the firm profits that can be targeted for remedial action

4 marks

2 (a)

Ratio	Description
Gross profit margin (%)	this shows the % of every £1 of sales that goes towards gross profit: $\dfrac{\text{gross profit}}{\text{sales}} \times 100$
Net profit margin (%)	this shows the % of every £1 of sales that goes towards net profit: $\dfrac{\text{net profit}}{\text{sales}} \times 100$
Mark up ratio	measure how much has been added to the cost of the goods as profit: $\dfrac{\text{gross profit}}{\text{cost of goods sold}} \times 100$
Return on capital employed	measure the return on the capital invested in the business by the owner of shareholder: $\dfrac{\text{profit before tax and interest}}{\text{total capital employed}} \times 100$

6 marks

(b)

GP Margin	<ul><li>increase sales revenue by increasing price or just number of sales</li><li>find cheaper suppliers</li><li>negotiate cheaper deals with existing suppliers</li><li>better stock management</li></ul>
NP Margin	<ul><li>increase gross profit</li><li>reduce expenses such as cut back on wages</li></ul>
Mark up ratio	<ul><li>find cheaper suppliers</li><li>negotiate cheaper deals with existing suppliers</li><li>increase sales revenue</li></ul>
ROCE	<ul><li>increase profit</li></ul>

4 marks

3 (a)

Ratio	Description
Current ratio	measures a firm's ability to pay its short term debts: $$\frac{\text{current assets}}{\text{current liabilities}}$$
Acid test ratio	measures a firm's ability to pay its short term debts in a crisis situation: $$\frac{\text{current assets} - \text{stock}}{\text{current liabilities}}$$

4 marks

(b)

Ratios	Ways to improve
Current ratio	• increase the firm current assets by obtaining finance through a bank loan or selling more goods on credit • reduce the current liabilities by paying off some short term creditors
Acid test ratio	• increase current assets relative to the current liabilities (stock cannot be altered as it is taken out of the equation) • reduce current liabilities relative to the current assets

2 marks

4 • they present historical information, it is out of date and only indicates to the firm what has happened in the past
  • the results are only valid when comparisons are made with firms which are in the same industry and are of similar size
  • results do not take account of internal factors such as staff morale
  • results do not take account of external factors such as a recession
  • the figures present a snapshot picture of the business and can fail to show product development

5 marks

2Fit Gym: Case Study 3

1 (a) This is a listing of all the firm's future receipts (cash inflows) and payments (cash outflows) over a period of time. All of the figures are predictions of what the firm will achieve. It is NOT the same as a cash flow statement.

2 marks

(b) • it allows the firm to see periods when they will have a cash surplus and so can plan to invest in the business at this time, e.g. refurbish the changing rooms
• a firm can also anticipate when they will be short of cash and so the necesary finance can be arranged such as an extension to the overdraft or a bank loan
• a cash flow is a necessary document to include in a business plan, which is the information submitted to a bank when attempting to secure a bank loan for a new venture or alteration to the business
• a cash flow allows a firm to keep its payments in line with its receipts and so avoid liquidity problems
• throughout the year the firm can add in its actual figures alongside the predicted ones and so gauge its forecasting abilities
• it helps the firm to set targets for departments or outlets

5 marks

2 A cash flow statement shows the uses of cash (e.g. purchasing some fixed assets) and sources of cash (e.g. allocation of shares) for a firm **for the previous year**(s).

2 marks

3 • employees – they wish to see if their jobs are secure as indicated by a good profit and if they are being paid a fair wage relative to the firm's profits
• bank – the bank will determine if the business is a viable option which allows them to gauge their level of risk and if it is worthwhile lending to them
• potential shareholders – they will be interested in the potential dividend from the business over the last trading year and if they should invest further and purchase more shares
• government – they will look at the accounts and confirm if the right amount of tax has been paid

• suppliers – they will look at the sales of the firm and determine if they are likely to receive future orders and future payments

5 marks

4 • the firm may show on its records that it has made £000s of sales so profits will be high, but in actual fact a large percentage of the sales have been sold on credit and the customers have not yet paid for them so cash will be low
• the firm may purchase a fixed asset such as a machine which is not shown on the profit and loss account as an expense, cash flow will appear reduced but profits will appear unchanged

2 marks

5 *Note: sources such as overdraft and trade credit are not acceptable for such a large investment.*

Bank loan:
• this can be quick to arrange and allows a firm to spread its repayments
• however, a small firm such as *2Fit Gym* may be charged a higher rate of interest

Share issue:
• this will involve *2Fit Gym* changing its status to a limited company
• this will allow large sums of money to be raised where repayments in the form of dividends are variable and can fall in line with the firm's profits

Debentures:
• this is a group of loans from other companies where the lenders become the debenture holders – this loan is normally for a period of around 25 years and the debenture holders receive fixed interest over the period of the loan and then receive the amount of the loan back at the end of the period
• if a firm declares a loss it must pay the debenture loan

Government grant:
• this involves the government agreeing to give a firm an agreed amount of funds which the firm is not expected to pay back

- however, the firm in not likely to receive a grant on a regular basis as it is competitive when seeking a grant and the council's funds are limited

Venture capitalist:
- this is also called a business angel (think of *Dragon's Den*) and they will often gives out loans where the banks have considered it too risky
- they will often demand a percentage of the business in return which lowers the owners return

6 marks

6 • responsible for compiling the relevant accounting documents such as a Profit and Loss Account or cash flow
   - ensure the correct payments are made on time to the appropriate parties
   - manage the credit of the firm ensuring all bills are chased on time

3 marks

Bootus: Case Study 1

1 • short notice for the interview
   - George had little time to prepare for the post
   - short interview where the manager did all the talking
   - George wasn't informed of his failure in the post till a month later

3 marks

2 • job Vacancy
   - job Analysis
   - job Description
   - person Specification
   - Advertise the post
   Note: VADSA

5 marks

3 • assess CVs
   - check references
   - interview the candidate
   - test the candidate such as with an aptitude test
   - inform the candidate whether they have the post or not

5 marks

4 • attainment tests – tests the candidate's skills such as words typed per minute. The candidates have to perform to a certain standard before they can be considered for the job
   - aptitude tests – candidates are tested on their natural abilities such as the ladder test with the fire brigade where staff are expected to perform certain tasks whilst at the top of a ladder
   - intelligence tests – measure a candidate's mental ability through tests such as numeracy or verbal reasoning. It demonstrates the persons ability to handle for example complex legal arguments or mathematical calculations for an engineering post
   - pyschometric tests – this attempts through, for example, questionnaires to reveal the candidate's traits or personality. This shows their ability to work in a team or take on a leadership role
   - medical – candidates are expected to reach a level of medical fitness that is essential for the job such as a fireman

8 marks

5 • the advert can be seen by a national audience
   - the firm can target the market segment that reads the paper
   - the advert can be seen by a large pool of external candidates
   - the advert has limited space to deliver the details
   - the advert has a limited shelf life, e.g. one day

4 marks

Bootus: Case Study 2

1 • tour of the factory
   - introduce line manager
   - receive health and safety training
   - receive a copy of the company manual
   - award any other appropriate suggestion, e.g. appoint a mentor

4 marks

2 (a) On the job training is being trained at your work place. *(Note simply saying you're at your work is not completely accurate.)*
Off the job training is being trained away from your place of work.

2 marks

(b) • shadowing a colleague
• coaching an employee
• observe an employee

3 marks

(c) • attend a college
• visit another firm perhaps owned by the firm, e.g. a *TopShop* employee could visit a *Dorothy Perkins* shop – both are owned by Arcadia
• attend a conference on your specialism
• take a DVD home
• visit the company's training centre

3 marks

3 *Note with explain questions you have to mention the consequence.*
• staff become more competent at their jobs and so quality improves
• staff acquire a wider range of skills and so can be more flexible and can be more mobile around the firm e.g. covering for absent colleagues
• staff motivation increases and so absenteeism is likely to fall
• the firm can improve its reputation and so attract better employees and also incur fewer accidents
• there is less waste and so the firm saves money

But:
• it can be costly and there is no guarantee they will have a return on their investment as the employee may leave soon after completing their training
• when staff are away being trained the firm may lose output and a fall in sales can result
• the training has to be of a high standard and relevant to the employee's job otherwise it is a waste of time

6 marks

4 (a) This is a review of the staff's performance over a period of time

1 mark

(b) • good practice can be acknowledged which motivates the employee
• training needs can be identified which raises quality standards
• the firm can ensure all its aims are introduced across all employees
• a bond is formed between manager and employee as they are forced to meet and agree on targets of mutual benefit to both parties
• wage increases are administered as they are based on performance which can be viewed as a fairer system

3 marks

5 • offer staff training
• organise social events
• teamwork
• quality circles
• staff rotation
• appraisals

3 marks

Bootus: Case Study 3

1 • sit-ins and strikes had occurred in the past
• owners refused to invite unions when negotiating wages
• staff had a lot of resentment to management
• staff were unwilling to accept changes in the workplace

4 marks

2 • sit in – where staff will remain at the workplace but refuse to carry out any work
• work to rule – involves staff only working the tasks detailed in their job descriptions – so extra duties volunteering for quality circles are banned
• go slow – where staff produce carry out their normal work but at a slower rate so output falls but normal wage levels are maintained

- overtime ban – where staff refuse to work any overtime which can prevent the firm from meeting an urgent order
- strike – where staff refuse to work and instead picket or demonstrate outside their place of work

4 marks

3
- consultation – managers can ask the opinions of staff before they introduce a change into the firm. These views can be collected via staff meetings or email surveys, for example
- arbitration – in times of a dispute with staff where an agreement cannot be reached, managers can call in an impartial judge, such as ACAS. They will rule on a dispute and the decision must be binding
- negotiation – instead of imposing a decision on staff, management can discuss an issue, such as pay increases, and both sides should be prepared to compromise
- quality circles – where workers volunteer to meet up in small groups with other workers and managers to discuss improvements to their work
- worker directors – involves workers sitting in a Board of Directors meeting to inform management of any issues. They are only consulted and have no voting rights on matters

5 marks

4
- speak to their line manager
- consult Human Relations department
- seek advice from their union
- contact ACAS for an impartial decision
- take industrial action such as a sit-in etc.

5 marks

5 *Health and Safety at Work Act 1974* demands the employer take reasonable care to uphold the health and safety of its employees. The employees must also take reasonable care to ensure they adhere to the instructions of their employers e.g wearing safety goggles when requested.

Equal Pay Act 1970 where the firm ensures any women undertaking the same, similiar or work of equal worth to a man is entitled to the same rate of pay and terms of employment.

Sex Discrimination Act 1975 where the firm ensures that it is unlawful to discriminate against an employee on the grounds of gender.

Race Relations Act 1976 where the firm ensures that it is unlawful to discriminate against a worker on the ground of race, colour, nationality or ethnic origins.

Disability Discrimination Act 1995 where the firm ensures that it is unlawful to discriminate against a worker due to their disability. So factors such as access to buildings have to be altered.

National Minimum Wage Act 1998 make it illegal for employers to pay their workers below the minimum wage level as set by the government for the relevant age band.

Offices, Shops and Railway Premises Act 1963 sets out the conditions that employers must abide by to ensure the safety and security of the workplace.

4 marks

6
- workers are reluctant to accept any changes and so the firm does not keep up with market trends
- the firm gains a bad reputation and so fails to attract good applicants for a post
- staff may take industrial action which could result in output being disrupted and so sales fall short of their target

3 marks

NAB 1: ChocOBloc

1 (a) private limited company

1 mark

(b)

Business	Ownership	Control	Finance
Tartan Chocs Ltd	shareholders	directors e.g. Lewis	share capital and list*
local authority/ council NHS	government	hospital board	government grants, taxes
voluntary/charity Oxfam	board of trustees	shop managers	donations, revenue from shops, grants and list*

*list = bank loan, bank overdraft, hire purchase, leasing, trade credit

6 marks

2 (a) **Strategic** decision – decision to focus on increasing sales
Justification – this would have been made by senior management and set out a vision for the firm against which all tactical decisions will be based. Also to grow/extend market share
Tactical decision – focus on the age group 14–21
Justification – this decision would enable the firm to focus their efforts effectively to achieve the strategic decision of maximising sales. Accept also changing the packaging/ launching a new ad campaign/introducing a new ICT system

4 marks

(b) *Award 1 mark for each objective.*
The firm may have an objective to simply break even in light of the poor economic climate but may have changed direction to increasing sales after their efforts to improve the business.

2 marks

3 Advantages:
- no rash decisions are made
- the firm takes time to consider alternatives solutions
- a logical process is followed which gives a structure to follow
- time is taken to evaluate the decision and gauge how effective it has been which will influence future decisions

Disadvantages:
- not all decision require such attention
- a gut reaction or intuition is overlooked which is a trait of many entrepreneurs
- production is lost whilst time is taken to walk through the decision model

6 marks

4 *Award 1 mark for each source and its example, maximum 2 marks and 1 mark for a valid point on reliability/value, maximum 2 marks per source.*
Note: watch for flips or repeats.

Source	Example
Primary	observation, telephone survey
Secondary	Mintel report
Internal	sales figures of staff, database of clients, spreadsheet report
External	Mintel report

Source	Reliability/Value
Primary	<ul><li>up to date</li><li>gathered for a specific purpose so relevant</li><li>can have its accuracy checked</li><li>can be time-consuming to collect</li><li>not always cost-effective as the response rates are low</li></ul>
Secondary	<ul><li>not always directly relevant</li><li>cheaper to collect than primary</li><li>wide range of sources often available</li><li>easy to access i.e. visit to the library</li><li>bias is difficult to check e.g. size of sample supporting article in the paper</li><li>often out of date</li></ul>
Internal	<ul><li>reliable as the source can be checked</li><li>relevant to the firm's needs</li><li>incomplete as it excludes competitor's results</li><li>sometimes expensive to set up systems to collate data e.g. Epos system for a small shop</li></ul>
External	<ul><li>gives an invaluable picture of the external environment</li><li>easy to get hold of and so is often cost effective</li><li>may contain bias which is difficult to verify</li><li>allows comparisons to be made with competitors</li></ul>

6 marks

5 (a)
- databases of clients were used to undertake primary research in the form of a telephone survey
- conference calls were used to discuss their findings
- spreadsheets were used to calculate the breakdown in sales for each region
- CAD system was used to design the packaging for the chocolate bar

4 marks

(b) Costs:
- financial cost of purchasing, installing and maintaining the equipment
- teething problems as equipment is being installed
- lost productivity as the staff are being trained to use the equipment
- reluctance of some staff to adopt the new systems

Benefits:
- reduction in errors
- may replace some staff which reduces costs
- fexibility of machines i.e. CAD design changes are easily transferred to CAM machines
- increased output so increased sales
- better ways of maintaining quality i.e. temperature controlled machines for making chocolate
- enhanced reputation of sophisticated production lines

6 marks

6 *The mark is gained only when the stakeholder AND influence are described.*
- customers may dislike the packaging and so it will have to change
- shareholders may seek better dividends which requires profits to be taken away from investment in other areas of the business such as advertising
- bank may refuse to grant *Tartan Chocs Ltd* a loan which means their expansion plans may have to be curtailed
- workers can object to the introduction of new technology for fear of losing their jobs and so this may delay its introduction in to the plant

- managers ability to make good decisions will influence the speed and effectiveness with which *Tartan Chocs Ltd* plans are introduced
- local community can generate good publicity for the firm by supporting expansion plans to the factory and granting permission for signs to be placed in the neighbourhood
- government may refuse planning permission for an expansion to the factory or introduce legislation that directly effects their wage levels, e.g. Minimum Wage Act
- suppliers can vary credit terms/ discounts with the firm which impacts directly on their profit levels

5 marks

NAB 2: ChocOBloc

1
- product – the brighter colours will appeal to a younger audience and hopefully separate it from the other brands on the market
- place – selling the chocolate in retail outlets that are visited by young people increases the firm's chances of reaching their target audience
- promotion – it is necessary for the firm to raise awareness of their brand name via the radio and then further endorsed via a billboard campaign where the consumers can see the product and are persuaded to buy
- price – this is the amount of money received by *Tartan Chocs Ltd* for their product. In this case it is priced alongside the leading brand so as to give the impression it is of the same quality

4 marks

2
- the introduction of brighter colours on the **product packaging** will fit in with the lively decor of the **place** is retail outlets like *Topshop* and *Apple*
- selling the products in trendy **places** for young people can be matched with **advertising** on radio channels that young people listen to and are sometimes played in the shops

- **promoting** the product via the radio can generate good sales to fund the change in **packaging** costs
- keeping the **price** in line with the competition ensures the **product** maintains an image of quality

2 marks

3 (a) *Allocate one mark for **describing** the segment and one mark for **justifying** its suitablility.*
- **age** – *ChocOBloc* could appeal to a younger audience e.g. 14–21, this could give them a niche market which increases the chances of inceased sales
- **income** – *ChocOBloc* could be given a high price to give the image of a luxury brand which is bought by people as gifts
- **hobbies** – *ChocOBloc* could be sold in vending machines in gyms and golf clubs as an energy bar which would attact anyone needing a sugar boost either before or after sport
- **gender** – *ChocoBloc* could be packaged in so-called "girly" colours to appeal to women who are big consumers of chocolate and so will guarantee the firm good sales

4 marks

(b) *1 mark for a clear explanation, single phrases will not be acknowledged.*
- the correct price can be established that is afforded by the group of consumers to whom the product is being directed
- promotions can be placed in mediums such as bus stops for students which increases their chances of exposure and increases the return and effectiveness of the promotional campaign
- the most appropriate channel of distribution can be used such as vending machines in colleges or schools to ensure the product is within reach of the target market

- the correct packaging can be designed to appeal to the selected audience and appropriate ingredients selected such as fizzy ingredients for young people and softer marshmallow products for an OAP audience
- research can focus on a specific group and so save costs and time collecting unnnecessary data on a group of consumers who are being targeted by the firm

4 marks

4 (a) *1 mark is given ONLY if an explantion is awarded. (1 mark each)*
- telephone/postal/street surveys
- group discussions
- hall test
- customer audits
- observation (e.g. CCTV)
- test marketing
- use of technology – EPOS/Loyalty cards/Digital TV

2 marks

(b) *1 mark given where a direct comparison is made.*
- field research is up to date whilst desk is often historical
- data collected is highly relevant to the issue in hand whilst desk research is often partially related and provides only a general comment on the matter
- the accuracy of the field research is easy to check such as a possible error in a questionnaire however checking such details in a published piece of information is problematic or virtually impossible
- field research is the private ownership of the firm whilst desk research is often on release to the general public and competitors

4 marks

5 *1 mark for a full explanation, one word responses will not be accepted.*
Tartan Chocs Ltd would be interested in the supplier's:
- prices or possible discounts for bulk purchases which impacts on costs

- credit terms on offer which helps spread *Tartan Chocs Ltd* repayments
- quality of goods which will influence how the product is viewed
- reliability to ensure late deliveries are not an issue
- ICT compatability to gauge if, for example, edi links can be established
- location to ensure the goods are not subject to time delays
- after sales service to ensure *Tartan Chocs Ltd* has someone on hand quickly should a problem arise

4 marks

6 (a) *Tartan Chocs Ltd* are using a batch method of production which allows the firm to halt production and change the ingredients or sizes of the bars to meet their requirements.

2 marks

(b) Batch v job:
- opportunities for some bulk purchases of raw materials which reduces costs
- less need for highly skilled staff which reduces costs
- opportunities for purchase of some production equipment that allows large batches to be produced and save costs
- each batch can be similar which allows for easier control of quality across a number of products
- larger quantities can be produced which generates larger sales

Batch v flow:
- batches can be changed which appeals to more market segments
- a greater variety is produced which allows for more individuality
- the variety in the products can allow for more pricing techniques and at times a higher price
- stocks of partly finished goods can be built up with allows a firm to respond quickly to market changes

4 marks

7 (a) • reduces the number of customer complaints
- reduces the number of mistakes and avoids costs associated with waste
- firm can charge a high price for the product
- builds up customer loyalty
- builds up confidence in the brand which makes it easier for the firm to launch a new product
- conforms to the industry standards for the production of chocolate

3 marks

(b) • costs of training managers to e.g. run quality circles
- initial slowing of production as quality checks are introduced which can lower output
- improved raw materials may cost more
- admin costs associated with the introduction of quality manuals and checking forms

4 marks

8 • the cost of labour to, for example, drive the vans
- the availability of intermediaries, e.g. retailers
- the geographical area covered by the clients
- the volume of products to be distributed
- the client demands, e.g. the supermarkets may wish delivery direct to the shops
- the firm's fleet of delivery lorries and their capability

3 marks

NAB 3: ChocOBloc

1 Finance function will:
- provide information to help managers to make decisions
- monitor the financial records and accounts of the firm to ensure there is enough money availabe to fulfil the firm's objectives

- prepare financial accounts such as the P&L account
- ensures payments are made in the form of wage and bills to creditors
- chase in unpaid bills and arrange a system of good credit control

3 marks

2 (a)

Ratio	
Gross profit as % of sales	This has risen possibly due to a rise in sales or a fall in the cost of goods sold as a result of changing to a cheaper supplier
Net profit as % of sales	This has fallen due to a possible rise in expenses or a fall in gross profit
Return on capital employed	This has risen meaning the firm is giving a better return on any capital invested
Current ratio	The ability of the firm to pay its short term debts has improved possibly due to an increase in current assets or reduction in current liabilities
Acid test ratio	The ability of the firm to cover its short term debts in a crisis is deteriorating, possibly due to the firm holding too much stock

4 marks

(b)

Ratio	
Gross profit as % of sales	The firm could increase its sales through an advertising campaign or reducing its cost of goods sold by changing to a cheaper supplier
Net profit as % of sales	The firm could reduce its expenses by cutting wages through banning overtime, or applying energy initiatives to cut fuel bills
Return on capital employed	Increase net profit or reduce its capital employed
Current ratio	The firm could increase current assets, for example, by increasing price or reducing the amount of stock being stolen or damaged
Acid test ratio	The firm could reduce its stock by increasing its sales. Increase its current assets or reduce its current liabilities

4 marks

3
- firm is dealing with historical information
- the firm must compare like for like otherwise the comparison is invalid
- the ratios do not account for external factors such as a recession
- the ratios do not account for internal factors such as low staff morale

4 marks

4
- the firm can note when it has surplus cash which dictates when it is appropriate to invest in new machinery, for example
- the firm can compare actual performance with its budgeted performance and gauge its forecasting abilities
- targets can be set for departments and managers
- a firm can see when it will have cash shortages and so remedial action can be taken
- it allows delegation of authority to managers without losing control

4 marks

5
- auditor role – monitor if HR policies, e.g. Health and Safety training has been given to all staff
- consultancy role – clarify any matters to do with HR, e.g. the correct ways to discipline a member of staff or the number of maternity days a worker is entitled to
- executive role – they provide senior management with information on whether a location could provide the necessary number of employees with the correct skill level
- service role – carry out HR tasks for departments such as first round interviews for posts
- facilitator role – they provide courses for staff training

4 marks

6 (a)
- a job vacancy is identified and analysed
- a job description is drawn up
- based on this information a person specification is compiled.
- the job is then advertised internally and externally
- the pool of candidates is selected
- CV and references are checked
- a first round of interviews takes place
- the candidates are tested using a variety of testing techniques
- the correct candidate is selected

4 marks

(b)
- the firm has to be assured it recruits the right person for the job
- it is costly to take people away from their posts to interview and so the right pool of candidates have to considered
- improves the firm's chances of recruiting someone who will remain with the firm for a long spell
- attracts the best candidates for the post

3 marks

7 Employee:
- staff are motivated as they can acquire more skills
- staff are prepared for future promotion
- staff become more confident to cope with change
- staff become more competent and so there are fewer mistakes

Employer:
- the quality of the firm's products should improve
- the firm finds it easier to introduce changes
- firm attracts a better quality of applicant
- staff can cover for each other and so productivity is not lost
- safety standards are maintained in the firm

6 marks

8
- Health and Safety at Work Act 1974 demands the employer take reasonable care to uphold the health and safety of its employees. The employees must also take reasonable care to ensure they adhere to the instructions of their employers e.g. wearing safety goggles when requested
- Equal Pay Act 1970 states that any women undertaking the same, similiar or work of equal worth to a man is entitled to the same rate of pay and terms of employment
- Sex Discrimination Act 1975 states that it is unlawful to discriminate against an employee on the grounds of gender

- Race Relations Act 1976 states that it is unlawful to discriminate against a worker on the ground of race, colour, nationality or ethnic origins
- Disability Discrimination Act 1995 states that it is unlawful to discriminate against a worker due to their disability. So factors such as access to buildings have to be altered

- National Minimum Wage Act 1998 make it illegal for employers to pay their workers below the minimum wage level as set by the government for the relevant age band
- Offices, Shops and Railway Premises Act sets out the conditions that employers must abide by to ensure the safety and security of the workplace

4 marks

Vocabulary Tests

Key

Pupil speak – where a definition is simplified for ease of understanding.

Exam tip – this is a guide to the depth or accuracy of your answer in order to get a mark in the exam.

Unit 1 Business in Contemporary Society

Limited liability

When the liability (responsibility) of a shareholder in a company is limited to the amount of investment (money, shares) of their orginal investment.

Pupil speak: in the event of the firm going bust the shareholder only stands to lose the value of their shares.

Tertiary Sector

In this sector of the economy, firms provide a service, e.g. banks, gyms, retailers (shops).

Publicly funded organisation

This is a type of organisation that is controlled by the government but owned by the taxpayer. They are not departments but instead trade services, e.g. BBC and the Bank of England.

Exam tip: don't confuse with a public limited company (PLC). This is a firm that sells shares on the stock market and is in the private sector.

Economies of scale

Achieved when the average costs of a firm fall when the firm increases output and size. Often achieved when a firm has the chance to bulk buy large quantities of a good.

Pupil speak: the cost savings a firm makes when it increases its size.

Exam tip: If describing this as an advantage to a firm, always use the example of bulk buying to secure you the mark.

Entrepreneur

An individual who develops an idea and combines the factors of production (i.e. land, labour, capital and enterprise) in order to produce a good or provide a service.

Exam tip: an entrepreneur is NOT someone who just thinks up the idea. They MUST put it into practice.

Franchisee

This is someone who pays the franchiser a fee to trade under their brand name. This fee can be a percentage of annual turnover or a set royalty payment. An example is *McDonalds*.

Exam tip: to avoid getting mixed up between franchisee and franchiser, some pupils think of the employee and employer.

Hire Purchase

This is a source of finance where a good (e.g. a machine) can be paid for through an initial deposit and then a series of installments, over a fixed period of time. After the last payment, the company takes ownership of the good (machine).

Exam tip: this is often confused with leasing which is the same set-up only the company doesn't own the machine at the end of the payment period. The word purchase is your guide.

Debentures

This a group of loans from individuals/ companies who become debenture holders (i.e. they hold onto the IOU's). The debenture holder receives fixed interest over the period of the loan and at the end of the loan period (often 25 years) they receive the amount of the loan back.

Exam tip: this source of finance is only used with large purchases such as building a medium to large size factory.

Diversification

This occurs when a business expands by moving into different markets, e.g. *Virgin* is involved in transport and television.

Outsourcing

This involves a firm sending out parts of its work to be carried out by another firm, e.g. a firm may hire another firm to carry out the cleaning, catering, accounting or legal aspects of its business.

Management buy-in

This involves a group of managers from outside the business who take over the firm and attempt to run it.

Exam tip: this is often confused with a management buy-out where managers from inside the business buy over control of the firm.

SME

This is a small to medium sized enterprise that employs 250 staff or less.

Unit 2 Business Information & ICT

Quantitative information

This is information that can be measured and is normally expressed in the form of numbers, e.g. '68% of our sample thought *Coca-cola* was better than *Pepsi*'.

Qualitative information

This information that is expressed in words and often reveals an opinion, e.g. one diner thought the service in the restaurant was intimidating (which could be interpreted as too pushy or isn't friendly).

E-commerce

This involves goods being sold via a company's website.

CAD

This stands for computer aided design. Note that it is software and is used to design, e.g. training shoes before the design is approved and sent to a factory in another part of the world for manufacture, using CAM (computer aided manufacture).

Sources of information

This is where the information is found e.g. from a primary source such as a questionnaire. The four sources are primary, secondary, internal and external.

Exam tip: pupils often get this mixed up with types of information, see next definition.

Types of information

This is what the information consists of, e.g. written, pictoral, graphical, numerical and verbal. Also qualitative and quantitative.

Unit 3 Decision-making in Business

Strategic decision

This is decision made by SENIOR management and sets out the VISION or strategic aim of the firm, e.g. to improve profits.

Exam tip: it is often general in nature. Don't get confused with a decision that will involve the senior managers of a firm but is in fact tactical, e.g. to launch a new product. The strategic decison here would have initially have been to "appeal to a new market segment". The firm would achieve this by launching a new product, e.g. *Nike* launching a training shoe for the elderly to attract new segment of buyers for their range of sports footwear.

Tactical decision

This decision is generally made by MIDDLE management and sets out how the firm will achieve its strategic objectives, e.g. if the strategic decision if to increase profits then the firm's tactical decision MAY be to increase price.

SWOT analysis

This is a model used by a firm to establish their current position in the marketplace. It will reveal the internal strengths and weaknesses and the external opportunties and threats that the firm faces.

POGADSCIE

This is a structured decision-making model that suggests the steps a firm should follow when undertaking a significant decision in the business.

Unit 4 Internal Organisation

Functional grouping

This is a way of grouping your staff, in this case it would be organising your firm by department where staff have similar skills and expertise.

Chain of command

This is the route through which an order passes as it is travels down an organisation chart.

Span of control

This the number of subordinates reporting directly to a manager.

Line manager

This is the manager directly above a worker on the organisation chart.

Hierarchy

The number of layers of authority in a firm's organisation chart.

Formal organisation structure

This explains the relationships between staff that have been prearranged by the firm, e.g. by department, level of authority and in terms of superiors and subordinates.

Informal organisation structure

This explains the relationships between staff that have not been prearranged by the firm. They are commonly found when socialising or during contact time away from the official place of work, e.g. the staffroom or the office five-a-side team.

Entrepreneurial structure

This is an organisation structure where the key decisions are made by a few people at the core of the firm.

Matrix

This is an organisation structure where project teams are formed to carry out specific projects. The members of each team would come from different functions.

Decentralised

Control and decision-making is delegated to different departments or branches of the firm.

Delayering

Removing a layer of authority or layer of management with the aim of flattening the organisation structure.

Downsizing

This involves a firm removing certain areas of the business by closing factories or merging firms together.

Empowerment

This involves a firm giving staff more responsibility for their own work often through delegation.

Corporate culture

This is the value, beliefs and norms relating to the company that are shared by all its staff.

Unit 5 Marketing

Product orientation

This is where a firm first manufactures a product and then tries to persuade customers to buy it.

Market segmentation

A firm would divide its customers into groups of customers with similiar characteristics, e.g. *Topman* will aim it products at young men, often students.

Niche market

This involves a firm aiming its products at a small segment of the market, e.g. *The Whisky Shop*.

Note: pupils often mix up the term small segment and small market. The shop is only aimed at whisky drinkers but the number of customers doesn't have to be small.

Undifferentiated marketing

This involves aiming products at the population as a whole, e.g. milk.

Consumer audit

This is a form of field research where the customer will keep a record of their buying habits of a product, often in diary. This information is then passed on to the market research company who will analyse the results.

Example: a teenager could keep a weekly record of their consumption of chocolate and report back to the market research firm via a phone survey.

Hall test

When firms invite a consumer to try their product and give their opinion on it, often via a small stall in a location such as a supermarket.

Random stratefied sampling

When selecting a sample of respondents the firm will ensure the profile of the sample matches the make-up of the population.

Example: if your population comprises of 40% from the C socio-economic group and 60% from the DE socio-economic group, then the firm would ensure, regardless of the actual number of respondents interviewed, that their sample was made up of 40% C and 60% DE.

Tip: A firm can simply ask their respondents their occupation to confirm which socio-economic group they would be placed into.

Product line extension

This involves a firm launching new variations to its original product, e.g. Peanut Kitkat.

Loss leaders

This pricing technique involves a firm lowering price often to an unprofitable level, to attract customers into the shop where more profitable goods would be purchased, e.g. own-brand bread.

Direct selling

Where a firm attempts to sell their products direct to the customer, e.g. often via the internet or catalogue.

In to the pipeline promotions

Where the manufacturer or wholesaler offers short term inducements to the other intermediaries to stock their products, e.g. staff training or point of sale materials such as small wire racks to display chewing gum near the tills.

Unit 6 Operations

System design

This is the activity where a manager decides on the layout of the factory to ensure the efficient flow of work between the different operation areas.

Purchasing mix

This collectively describes the factors a manager would consider before deciding on a supplier. These factors include reliability, location of the suppliers's premises and price being charged.

Computerised stock control system

The system by which stock is controlled electronically by an automatic trigger system. When stock falls below a preset level an order is automatically raised, sent to the supplier and stock levels return to their maximum level. These levels are calculated by average daily usage rates.

JIT

This is where stock is delivered to the factory just in time for it to be put onto the production line. A firm would have the aim of zero stocks.

Commission

This is a form of payment system where an employee is paid a wage as based on the value of the sale they have made, e.g. if a salesman has a £1000 sale and their commission is 10% then they will receive £100 towards their salary.

Capital intensive production

This is a term given to a firm where the organisation has a greater proportion of machines to labour. It is common to a manufacturing plant such *Tunnocks* or *Ford* cars.

Benchmarking

A firm will set their quality goals to match those of the market leader.

Quality assurance

A firm will check the quality standards of their production at certain points in the production line.

Exam tip: this term is often confused with quality control where quality is checked before the goods are sent out to the retailers.

Distribution mix

This is all the factors that are considered when deciding on the route through which a manufacturer distributes the product. The factors to be considered are desired image for the product, finance etc.

Unit 7 Financial Management

Gross profit

This is the profit calculated when the cost of sales are subtracted from the sales revenue.

This is calculated in the trading account.

Net profit

This is the profit made when the expenses are subtracted from the gross profit. This is calculated in the profit and loss account.

Fixed asset

This is an item which the firm owns and will keep for more than one year, e.g. machinery and premises.

Current liability

This represents something the firm owes and will pay for within the year.

Debtors

These are customers who have still to pay for goods received.

Exam tip: pupils often get mixed up between debtors and creditors. Think of buying goods on credit where the firm would receive goods and pay for them later.

Creditors

Suppliers who the firm owes money to.

Working capital

This represents the funds the firm has left after it has subtracted their current liabilities (bills it owes) from their current assets (items it owns).

Pupil speak: it shows the firm how much funding it has to work with on a daily basis.

Drawings

These are funds taken out by the owner from the firm for their own personal use.

Liquidity

This shows a firm's ability to pay their short term debts.

Net profit margin

This measure the percentage of every £1 of sale that goes towards net profit.

Acid test ratio

This shows the firm's ability to pay their short term debts in a crisis situation.

Cash budget (cash flow forecast)

This is a financial document that charts the money coming into the firm (receipts) and the money leaving the firm (payments).

Unit 8 Human Resource Management

Job description

This is part of the recruitment process and details the job title, location, tasks, duties and responsibilities of the vacant post.

Person specification

This is part of the recruitment process and details the type of person suitable for the post, including the desired qualifications, experience, character traits and interests.

Aptitude test

This is part of the selection process and it tests a candidates natural abilities such as a fireman's ability to handle fire equipment whilst at the top of a ladder.

Induction training

This is training given to a new recruit in a firm.

Note: every new recruit, regardless of age, is given a form of induction training, so a new headteacher would receive induction training.

Off the job training

Where training is undertaken away from the worker's place of work.

Job rotation

This is where a trainee moves around different departments or jobs to achieve an overview of the firm.

Appraisal

This is a review of a worker's performance against agreed targets, by a manager, over a period of time.

Arbitration

This is where a firm would seek the services of an impartial judge in the event of a dispute. This judge is often ACAS, who are regarded as neutral and don't stand to benefit from the outcome of the dispute.

Go slow

This is a form of industrial action where workers produce work at a slower rate than normal, perhaps by following all procedures mentioned in a manual.